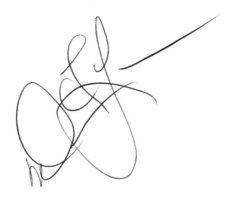

Rustproof Relationships

A Guide to Healthy Relationships and Effective Coping Skills

**Diana F. Lee, M.Ed., M.P.A.,
PMC Transforming Spirituality**

Edited by Stanley D. Wilson Ph.D.

ISBN: 1466466375
ISBN-13: 9781466466371
Library of Congress Control Number: 2011919205
CreateSpace Independent Publishing Platform
North Charleston, South Carolina

Diana F. Lee, M.Ed., M.P.A.,
PMC Transforming Spirituality
Author of:

Touching the Soul: a therapeutic guide to spiritual and personal growth

And the day came when the risk it took
to remain tightly closed in a bud
was more painful than the risk it took to bloom.

—Anaïs Nin

Acknowledgments

The hardest part of writing this book was finishing it, which took me nearly three years. There are a number of people I would like to thank for assisting in the delivery. Much appreciation to my wonderful editor, Stanley Wilson, Ph.D., a friend who has spent much creative time and effort with me in discussing and honing the ideas I have passed along to my readers. I'd also like to mention Lee Nye, Ph.D., The Rev. Linda Kaufman, MBA, MDiv; PMC Transforming Spirituality, B.C.C., Sue Keacher, M.Ed., Kathryn Anderson, Andrea Adams, D.N., Steve Olsen, N.D., Anthony Zecca, Sarah Burchfield, Darrell Lee, M.Ed., William Taylor (supportive husband), and Katherine Lee Taylor (beloved daughter), all of whom have spent time and energy giving me feedback about my raw manuscript. Many of my clients have made positive suggestions on the information that now appears in this book and have thus contributed to its development. A special acknowledgment is reserved for Angela Chase who has been dedicated to this project and made a number of creative contributions.

Dedication

To my many mentors who have shared their wisdom and guidance with me. Also to those teachers and friends who have helped me along the way—especially Marilyn Conaway (teacher at Bothell High School), Katherine Nelson, M.D., Jess Roebuck, M.D., Judge John Lawson, Professor Naomi Goodard (Seattle University), Professor Merdesces Hensley (University of Washington) and Professor Valerie Lesniak (Seattle University).

Introduction

In this volume of *Rustproof Relationships: A Guide to Healthy Relationships and Effective Communication Skills*, I focus on relationship skills and communication tools. People are hurting. They struggle unsuccessfully with difficult thoughts, painful emotions, traumatic memories, and failed relationships.

I wrote this book because I used to be one of those people, so caught up in life's struggles that at one time I questioned whether I could go on. My job was unfulfilling, and I felt trapped in an endless pattern of addictive and abusive relationships. I felt inadequate, unable to turn my life around.

I decided to do something different, learn new skills and new ways of thinking and relating. I made a conscious choice to acquire skills that would equip me for real and lasting change. Along the way I discovered that coping skills are the tools necessary for handling the stresses of modern life and skillful communication is the way I connect in meaningful ways with others.

Thirty-eight years of successful teaching in the counseling profession has shown me I could educate others about what I'd learned. For the last eleven years I have used three therapy dogs (Brussels Griffons) in my practice. I have used Dr. Jerry, Jack, and Jenny to teach boundary skills along with many other skills that are included in this book. Once clients were taught how to cope they could tap into their native intelligence, develop their creativity, achieve their goals and navigate life's ups and downs without falling apart during the tough times.

Rustproof Relationships: A Guide to Healthy Relationships and Effective Communication Skills teaches the skills imparted and role-modeled by effective counselors and psychotherapists. These skills should have been taught in childhood, but weren't because parents and their parents never learned nor mastered them. People who lack communication and coping skills are infinitely more vulnerable and less happy. During tough times, their lives spin out of control, and they suffer negative thoughts and emotions such as chronic depression, worry, and shame. Worse yet, they relate unskillfully and end up frustrated and lonely, unable to secure the love they need. This book is about how to move from feeling overwhelmed and inadequate to living life to its fullest potential.

On Using This Book

This book is different. Typical self-help books tell you what's wrong with you, but neglect to offer any real solutions or lasting change. This one contains stories and examples that make up a primer for essential communication and coping skills. Clear directions and easy-to-follow worksheets make the process of change a positive experience. Each chapter builds self-awareness and a new perspective that gives birth to a choice: continue to struggle through life with an insufficient skill-set or succeed by trying out the suggestions placed throughout this book.

To get the most out of your reading experience, do one chapter at a time and participate in all the exercises. Find a safe and comfortable place to do the exercises, free from distractions. Be bare-bones honest with yourself and prepare for change. Recognize that even the so-called "negative" emotions provide feedback, yielding information that will guide you as you navigate your internal and external worlds.

Part One, "Relationship Skills," gives you tools such as how to recognize a safe person, fixing a "broken picker," dealing successfully with sexuality and intimacy. This section will better equip you with skills that will get you the love you want and deserve.

Part Two, "Communication Tools," talks about setting limits, praising others effectively, and dealing with annoying people. The proper way to set boundaries is discussed – an approach that actually works every time. You will learn to be a more effective listener and connect meaningfully with others.

COMING SOON: *Rustproof Relationships Revisited: A Guide to Personal Growth and Achieving Your Dreams and Goals*

My follow-up book is divided into two parts, as follows:

Part One, "Personal Growth," looks at important issues such as lifting depression, cooling the flames of anger, building positive self-esteem, learning to forgive, grieving the lost years, spotting the difference between grieving and whining, managing emotional triggers, and making mistakes skillfully.

Part Two, "Reaching Dreams and Goals," helps you put an end to procrastination, learn to manage perfectionism, deal with being overwhelmed and scattered, learn to keep dreams alive, handle job stress, and achieve your goals.

About The Examples In This Book

None of the examples presented in this book reflect the life experiences of any one individual. Rather, each is a composite formed from the lives of numerous people I have known. By using composites, changing names, and altering the stories I have heard and experienced, I am protecting the confidentiality of others. Any resemblance between anyone I have known and a real person is coincidental.

A note about pronouns; throughout the book, I use "he" in quotes or "she" in quotes interchangeably to refer to the typical Child or Adult. Any gender reference in the text is equally applicable to either gender. Using the more modern and generic "he/she" feels unnatural to the flow of thought. Hence the reader may assume that, unless otherwise stated, any reference to one gender, also holds true for the other. Having stated that, most of the examples concern women as this book is intended primarily for women.

Table Of Contents

Part One
RELATIONSHIP SKILLS

For a New Beginning

In out-the-way places of the heart,
Where your thoughts never think to wander,
This beginning has been quietly forming,
Waiting until you were ready to emerge.

For a long time it has watched your desire,
Feeling the emptiness growing inside you,
Noticing how you willed yourself on,
Still unable to leave what you had outgrown.

It watched you play with the seduction of safety
And the gray promises that sameness whispered,
Heard the waves of turmoil rise and relent,
Wondered would you always live like this.

Then the delight, when your courage kindled,
And out you stepped onto new ground,
Your eyes young again with energy and dream,
A path of plentitude opening before you.

Though your destination is not yet clear
You can trust the promise of this opening;
Unfurl yourself into the grace of beginning
That is at one with your life's desire.

Awaken your spirit to adventure;
Hold nothing back, learn to find ease in risk;
Soon you will be home in a new rhythm,
For your soul senses the world that awaits you.

—John O'Donohue

1
How To Recognize A Safe Person

Every time you don't follow your inner guidance, you feel a loss of energy, loss of power, a sense of spiritual deadness.

—Shakti Gawain

Men are not necessarily more selfish than women, but most of them truly are more self-centered.

—Helene G. Brenner, Ph.D.

Choosing a "safe person" to be in your life is not easy. Many of us either grew up with or became desensitized to unsafe behavior. We came to believe it is the norm. This tricks us into believing bad behavior is tolerable.

If you're considering someone to include in your circle of friends or as a potential relationship partner, talk to them and get a sense of their willingness to accept responsibility for their personal issues. Some will fall short of taking real responsibility. They can acknowledge a problem, but are unwilling to do anything about it. For example, I've heard men say, "I know I have a bad temper . . . that's just the way I am." Similarly, women will say, "I know I can be critical, but men are just so clueless!" Neither truly accepts responsibility. The "it's just the way I am" and "blame the other" arguments are both a cop-out.

Perhaps worse, some people present themselves as if they have no issues at all. Every disagreement and conflict is automatically your fault. Consider such an assertion a big "red flag" and find someone safer, someone more in touch with reality.

The idea in assessing safety is to be curious about any new person's family, relationships, and life history. You don't need to do a clinical interview or subject them to an interrogation, but in the course of getting to know them you can ask a few pertinent questions and see how they respond. What kind of family background do they have? What are their values and greatest strengths? Did the person complete their educational goals and find productive, gainful employment? Have they married? As you ask questions, the way the other answers will tell you if you're being intrusive. If they are open and disclosing, you can reciprocate and build trust. If you give them time and they are still unwilling to share their story or make any intimate self-disclosures, this could be a sign the relationship won't work in the long run. Remember, people are multi-dimensional, so even good people have faults. Finding faults doesn't mean you should trash the relationship, only that you should proceed with caution.

A psychologist colleague consulted with me on a client we will call Becky. Becky met Hannah at a quilting party and thought she'd made a new friend. At first, Hannah was friendly and supportive and the two did things together, but as the relationship continued, Becky began to feel intruded upon. For example, Hannah would call every day and ask about Becky's schedule, then act hurt if she wasn't included. On one occasion, Hannah came over uninvited and let herself in the house when Becky was upstairs in the shower. Becky was shocked by her friend's boldness and tried to set limits, but Hannah became defensive, denied any wrongdoing and even played the victim. The final straw occurred when Hannah insisted on purchasing new placemats for Becky after being told in no uncertain terms not to do so. At this point, Becky returned the placemats to Hannah and ended their developing friendship, explaining to Hannah that she could not be her friend because boundaries were not being respected. Becky regretted losing a friend, but realized that with no boundaries there was no safety.

A main goal of recognizing and choosing safe people is to avoid being hurt or victimized. If you notice your new friend is undependable (he promises to phone you after work and doesn't) or violates boundaries (he pressures you for sex when you've made clear you're not ready) or raises red flags (you go to dinner and he orders a triple margarita), you are entitled to express your concerns. Ask a few nosy questions to be certain you're not setting yourself up. If you don't get satisfactory answers, then ask yourself: "Is this person capable of a mature relationship based on trust and closeness?" "How much should I be involved with this person and in what way?" If we're talking about someone you're already involved with, you can still apply the same approach.

Everyone has issues that need resolution. We all have holes in our socks. Safe people readily admit their problems and work on them. Unsafe people deny their problems and try to export them to those who are willing to take on someone else's issues. If you are in a relationship with an unsafe person, you will lose your energy, time, self-esteem, and inner peace. Maybe even your sanity!

People have the capacity to grow and change, but if there are too many small issues or one important one that continues without resolution, consider whether your relationship is toxic or nurturing. Without safety, you will not get your needs met in the long run. Moreover, you may ultimately find yourself feeling abused or traumatized unless you pay attention to what makes an intimate partner or personal friend a safe one.

Here are twenty key traits of safe people. This list is not the final word, but a decent starting point. Read it carefully and reflect on important people in your past and present. How do they measure up? How do *you* measure up?

1. **Effective listener.** He doesn't interrupt when you are expressing yourself and knows how to validate your feelings. He not only "gets you," he is able to show you he understands. He offers support when you need it and asks questions like: "How would you like to be supported?" He doesn't automatically try to "fix" your problem without asking first if you want feedback. For example, if you were discussing a stressful day at work, he might just listen or offer a hug.

2. **Validates your perceptions.** Safe people do not "reality tamper" with your perceptions. Instead, they validate what you're thinking and feeling, even if it makes them anxious. Example: You are certain your new girlfriend is still sleeping with her ex-husband. She denies it, but you have evidence. This is crazymaking to you. She is willing

to distort reality and mess with your mind so she can deny reality. Proceed with caution!

3. **Able to express feelings**. He is in touch with his feelings and able to show them in an appropriate way. This means he is aware of his emotional life and can acknowledge and express joy, sadness, fear, anger, or shame when such feelings arise. Without this trait, people are not really equipped to handle the demands of intimate relationships.

4. **Sense of humor.** High on any list of what to look for in a friend or partner is a good sense of humor. Humor is one of our most effective coping skills and can infuse a relationship with a sense of playfulness and fun. Some unsafe people use humor to ridicule, control, or abuse. If you encounter this problem, call it to the person's attention and set a limit. If it keeps happening, end the relationship.

5. **Nonjudgmental regarding mistakes.** She shows support and encouragement on learning about the mistakes you make. She doesn't lecture you or pass on negative criticism. Example: You admit you backed the car out of the garage without first opening the garage door. Instead of berating you for being a knucklehead, she either empathizes or shares something "stupid" she did when she was in a hurry.

6. **Allows you to clean up your own mistakes.** He stays out of your business and offers support without being judgmental. Example: You are in a salary dispute at work and come on too strong with the boss. Your approach backfires. Instead of telling you what you should have said or done, he asks how he can best be supportive. He gives feedback or suggestions only if that's what you request.

7. **Owns their own mistakes.** He is mature enough to own up to mistakes and secure enough to admit to personal issues that need work. Example: You have your first fight with him and he loses his temper, calling you a "bitch" and storming from your home. Half an hour later he phones to apologize and the next day enrolls in

an anger management class. If he makes progress, he deserves a second chance.

8. **Competent in self-care.** She is mature and resourceful and doesn't become dependent on you. In other words, she lives consciously and takes responsibility for her own life, including her physical and mental health, personal and financial problems. If your new friend provides continuous situations for you to enable or rescue her, look out! If you have a need to rescue ("bird with a broken wing syndrome"), volunteer at the local animal shelter.

9. **Reasonably ordered life.** If you hook up with a guy who is continually in crisis, you're going to suffer needlessly. Some people attract chaos, and life becomes an endless series of stressors, betrayals, financial problems, lawsuits, and fights. The drama is a way of keeping the focus on the outside, guaranteeing they never have to deal with their real issues. Chaos is contagious. Beware.

10. **Self-sufficient.** She has her own self and doesn't get "lost" in you. Because her life is active and fully developed, she doesn't need to be "joined at the hip" with you. The two of you can do things independently, then come together and share. She finds her own path rather than presenting herself as dependent and helpless, trying to get you to tell her what to do.

11. **Clearly communicates expectations.** He is able to express his expectations, including his needs and his ideas regarding the direction of the relationship. As issues come up, he defines his boundaries and deals with issues as they arise. Example: He makes it clear he doesn't want you to spend the night at his home until his seventeen-year-old daughter has left for college.

12. **Reasonable expectations.** He is not a perfectionist who projects unrealistic expectations on you. He does not always need to be right and in control. He is not so selfish and immature that he

expects you to work full-time, raise the kids, and have dinner ready when he gets home.

13. **Flexible and open-minded.** He can be open about ideas, opinions, values, people, politics, religion, or ways to do things. That he is tolerant does not mean he is wishy-washy. Politically, he might be a passionate liberal, but he is willing to listen to and be curious about a more conservative point of view. He realizes his eyes are not God's eyes and can "agree to disagree" without needing to make you wrong.

14. **Understands boundaries.** When appropriate, he sets limits and boundaries both mindfully and with grace. Example: You become over-involved in disciplining his teenage daughter from a previous marriage. He listens to your point of view and is receptive to suggestions, but kindly asks you to allow him to handle this delicate situation. Similarly, he supports you in regard to the boundaries you set and doesn't experience them as abandonment, rejection, or criticism.

15. **Respectful.** He treats with respect those matters he may not understand or like, but that are important to you. He is never verbally, physically, or emotionally abusive. If he calls you names, curses at you, threatens you, shoves you, slaps your face, or forces you to participate in sexual acts against your will, run (do not walk) away from the relationship. Without respect, there can be no real connection or closeness.

16. **Honest and trustworthy.** This one is so simple and yet so very important. He tells the truth and his word means something. He lives with integrity, and you can trust his motives and actions. Example: A man you meet online tells you he only dates one woman at a time and after the third date he tells you he has removed his profile from the dating service. Only he hasn't. Red flag! If you lay down with dogs, you get up with fleas.

17. **Self-honesty.** He is not "in denial" about important issues. You notice a man you've been dating regularly misses a lot of work because he is hung-over from drinking with his buddies. You confront him and he becomes defensive, telling you it has only happened twice in the past year. You know better. There's an elephant in the room with you. If he is unwilling to acknowledge the problem, cut your losses by ending the relationship.

18. **Stable moods.** While we are all prone to an occasional meltdown, this trait refers to having a pattern of stable moods over time. This means he has reasonably good coping skills and does not fall apart during stressful times. People with severe mood swings often abuse others or leave them in crisis. If he has a problem, he will acknowledge it and get help via counseling and/or medication. Instability leads to violence.

19. **Clean and sober.** Sobriety is needed to sustain a safe and intimate relationship. If you find yourself involved with someone who abuses drugs or alcohol, confront him and see if he is willing and able to take responsibility for change. Be very careful how close you get to someone who is actively abusing substances. If you have any addictive issues, be certain your new friend is not an enabler who would compromise your recovery. Help is out there. No one needs to tackle this problem alone.

20. **Comfortable giving and receiving.** He can give you his time, effort and love, as opposed to some needy men who seemingly only take. He is also comfortable receiving, accepting your gifts of love in a way that establishes a relationship based on reciprocity. Example: After several months of dating, you notice he is only interested in getting together when he wants sexual gratification. As a habitual taker, he is not safe.

How To Recognize A Safe Person Worksheet

Everyone has issues that need work. Safe people take ownership and work on their issues. Rate your prospective friend or partner in accord with the key traits of safe people and take note of issues that need to be worked on.

A=Best
B=Good
C=Fair
D=Poor

1. Effective listener. ____

_____
_____

2. Validates your perceptions. ____

_____
_____

3. Able to express feelings. ____

_____
_____

4. Sense of humor. ____

_____
_____

5. Nonjudgmental regarding mistakes. ____

_____
_____

6. Allows you to clean up your own mistakes. ___

_____

_____

7. Owns their own mistakes. ___

_____

_____

8. Competent in self-care. ___

_____

_____

9. Reasonably ordered life. ___

_____

_____

10. Self-sufficient. ___

_____

_____

11. Clearly communicates expectations. ___

_____

_____

12. Reasonable expectations. ___

_____

_____

13. Flexible and open-minded. ___

_____

_____

14. Understands boundaries. ___

_____

_____

15. Respectful. ___

_____

_____

16. Honest and trustworthy. ___

_____

_____

17. Self-honesty. ___

_____

_____

18. Stable moods. ___

_____

_____

19. Clean and sober. ___

_____

_____

20. Comfortable giving and receiving. ___

_____

_____

Additional Comments:_____

_____

_____

_____

_____

In summary, obviously, there are many traits that determine how safe someone is. Let's examine how the worksheet is used in real life. Tamara, a recently divorced project manager in her mid-thirties, met Harold through an online dating service. They had long telephone conversations and exchanged numerous emails and text messages prior to meeting for coffee. The two hit it off, sharing a love of good literature and a passion for vacationing in warmer climes. For the first three months of their relationship, Harold seemed tender, sensitive, and attuned to Tamara's wants and needs. She was especially pleased to be with someone who was her intellectual equal. It looked like she had proven the old adage, "you only have to get lucky once!"

As the relationship appeared promising, Tamara agreed to rate Harold on the "safe person" worksheet. She gave him high marks on most of the twenty items, however, to Tamara's surprise, she realized he only earned a "C" on "effective listener," "able to express feelings," and "validates your perceptions." Until she put pen to paper, she said she would have given him an "A" or a "B" on all three. Number 14, "understands boundaries," was her greatest concern, and she had to rate him "D" – "Poor." The main reason was that Harold enjoyed telling off-color jokes with a sexual theme and persisted in doing so even after she made it clear she didn't appreciate such humor. And, on one occasion, he made a scene in a restaurant by insulting a waitress because his food wasn't properly prepared. Still, Tamara overlooked these few worksheet minuses because they were outweighed by all the pluses. Things unraveled on a trip to a resort in Mexico. At dinner, Harold berated Tamara for putting too much salt on a tomato, on the veranda he criticized her for reading a cheap novel, and on the beach he chastised her for crossing her legs in the sun ("you won't tan evenly"). His behavior was similarly inappropriate in the hotel room. When she refused a sexual favor he requested, he gave her the silent treatment. When she called attention to the distance and tension between them, he called her "ridiculous" and implied she was suffering from PMS, refusing to even discuss his behavior or her feelings about it.

On returning from the trip, Tamara re-took the worksheet test and found Harold lacking in many key traits of a safe person. She realized he'd been putting on a good front and that she'd allowed herself to be duped. I'd like to tell you she promptly jettisoned him from her life, but she didn't. It took another six months of working through her father wounds before she could find the self-respect and courage to end the relationship. To this day, she credits the worksheet exercise as the resource that gave her the self-awareness of what exactly was wrong with Harold and how important it was to demand safety.

The "safe person" worksheet can be used as a screening tool for any relationship. It can also be used as a discussion tool when considering a new partnership, or ending an old one. Your emotional and physical safety are at stake. What could be more important?

2
Broken Pickers, Making Repairs

Somewhere, somehow, someone must have
Kicked you around some
Who knows, maybe you were kidnapped
Tied-up, taken away, and held for ransom

—Tom Petty

It is especially easy for people to transfer their feelings about their parents
onto their partners, because, through a process of unconscious selection, they
have chosen partners who resemble their caretakers.

—Harville Hendrix

Dr. John Gottman, renowned for his research in the areas of marital stability and divorce prediction, made a surprising finding about what makes couples happy and likely to stay together. His research allowed him to predict with 90 percent accuracy the newlyweds who will stay married and those who will divorce within six years. Surprisingly, it is not the oft-quoted issues of money, sex, children, or in-laws that predict marital bliss or discord. It is the answer to the question, "Do you let your partner influence you?" Partners need to preserve their own identities, but they also need to yield to the other on certain issues.

According to Dr. Gottman, the most predictive variable of all is the answer to the question, "Does the man accept influence from the woman?" Men who are mature and secure enough to accept influence have happy partners and wives. Now the issues around money, sex, in-laws, and children take on new meaning. Suppose, for example, hubby wants to buy a powerboat, but you explain that the family finances simply can't handle an extra payment. If he drives home the next day with the boat in question hitched to his truck, Gottman would predict you will be one of the couples who either divorce or end up miserable. Conversely, if your partner wants sex eight times a week and you only want it once, but he accepts your compromise of twice a week without displays of anger or pouting, this would predict staying together and being happy. In other words, you don't have to give up yourself to be loved by a man, but you do have to pick a man who will let you influence him.

Denise believes she's found the perfect man, only to discover he flirts with her best friend. Denise asks him to stop, but he doesn't accept her influence. He either cannot or will not allow her to have influence through her power, a signal of his disrespect for her on a deep level. A month later she learns he cheated on her when he was out of town on a business trip. Making matters worse, it's a pattern for Denise. Her last boyfriend did pretty much the same thing. Is it just bad luck? No, Denise has a broken picker. The part of her that chooses a mate is asleep at the switch. Rather than watching for red flags to ensure her safety and security, her need to be in a relationship overrides her common sense (see chapter on *How to Recognize a Safe Person*).

Like a new car that rolls off the assembly line, each of us comes equipped with an impressive list of features, not the least of which is the most complicated and efficient on-board computer ever devised (our human brain). Our brains weigh only 3 pounds, yet miraculously house 1 billion neurons (the building blocks of the nervous system). Though we're wired for health and the ability to take in what nurtures us, our vehicles suffer wear and tear and, on the highway of relationships, this means we often end up with a broken picker. Having one doesn't mean we're bad or at fault, it just means we are likely to keep making the same mistakes unless we commit to some much-needed repair work.

To fix a picker you must become more aware of your pattern in choosing partners who aren't right for you. Back to Denise, who has suffered through numerous failed relationships in her two years of treatment with me. She picks men who are exciting and even a bit dangerous, but they're phobic about making long-term commitments. What follows is a transcript (modified to preserve client anonymity) of a session where we worked on Denise's self-defeating pattern. The conversation picks up where she's told me of meeting a man who approached her coming out of a restaurant. At this point, she's dated him for two weeks. She's learned he has no job, but plenty of money. When she tries to get any information as to how he supports himself, he becomes evasive.

DL: What was it like for you when he asked for your number?

Denise: I felt awkward, but really flattered. I mean . . . I know I shouldn't have given it to him, but he was attractive to me in that bad boy way that sucks me in. So I did it even though part of me said I was asking for trouble.

DL: It almost sounds like you didn't experience a choice. Like you felt compelled to give him your number even though you knew better.

Denise: That's true. Once he told me he thought I was cute and that he'd like to get to know me, it's like my willpower went right out the window.

DL: Like you've got a big doorbell and he just walked right up and rang it.

Denise: Yes! Exactly. He rang it, and I opened the door.

DL: (long pause) Here's where I am with you, Denise. I don't know if it will be interesting to you or if you can make use of it, but I'm thinking . . . she can't seem to disconnect her wiring so she's still attracted to these bad boys, but she didn't have to open the door.

Denise: You mean I should hear the doorbell chime, but ignore it.

DL: Not exactly ignore it, more like pay close attention to it and carefully consider how to respond. Make a conscious choice. I know this sounds motherly, but didn't anyone ever teach you not to open the door to strangers?

Denise: Are you mad at me?

DL: No, I'm not mad. But I am concerned. I like you a lot and I've seen this happen before . . . quite a few times . . . where you get involved with one of these commitment-phobic men, and then you get really hurt. I want you to consider driving with your headlights on.

Denise: (laughs) Yeah, I've got a light out.

Indeed, Denise has a light out, and it has cost her. In a year of therapy we have dealt with intense emotional pain, financial losses incurred by loaning money to deadbeat boyfriends, and even physical health consequences (she suffered a fractured collarbone as a result of domestic violence). I used to think competent mental health professionals could sort of rewire a client's brain and eliminate these unhealthy attractions to the wrong mates. Over the years I've come to believe some attraction burrows its way into the marrow of our bones, so the doorbell still chimes no matter how many times we learn the painful lesson. Now I teach my clients to use the chime as a clarion call, a warning of imminent danger. With awareness you can make an intelligent choice, and you then have the possibility of picking a mate with whom you can share a happy life. Repairing your picker is a necessary step if you are to enjoy a meaningful primary relationship.

So, if you're in the early stages of dating with a man who has shown he will not allow you to influence his behavior, hoist the red flag and either resolve the issues to your satisfaction or get the heck out of Dodge. Get out your checklist (below) and make sure you're not settling for less than you deserve and need. No woman gets the whole enchilada because there are no perfect men, but there are a lot of good-enough men out there who want to be in a meaningful and committed relationship.

To fix Denise's broken picker, I urged her to take responsibility by being discerning and looking for the following traits:

1. **Emotional stability:** Holds together under stress. No active addictions or is in recovery. Has a strong sense of self.
2. **Good physical health:** Healthy diet and regular exercise, gets medical help when needed.
3. **Balanced life:** Able to work, love, and play with skill.
4. **Sense of humor:** Can laugh at self and find humor in life.
5. **Communicates effectively:** Open, honest, direct, and listens.
6. **Problem-solving ability:** Can dialogue to work through problems.
7. **Creates a safe space:** Is honest, dependable, trustworthy, and supportive.

8. **Good friend:** Not just to you, but to others.
9. **Maturity:** Not resentful or threatened by your success. Financially responsible. Doesn't let the Inner Child run the show.
10. **Compatible values, goals, and priorities:** Value driven. Honors different opinions.
11. **Honesty:** Integrity and dependability with self and others. Not phony or manipulative.
12. **Respectful:** Interested in your opinion, even if disagrees. Has healthy boundaries. Honors your boundaries.
13. **Romantic:** Can give and receive without constant reminders.
14. **Spiritual:** Can connect from the heart and soul.
15. **Sexual compatibility:** Similar interests and appetite, negotiable.
16. **Child rearing:** Share healthy, similar philosophy.
17. **Compatible lifestyle:** Able to negotiate city/country, boat/condo/house, children, animals, and tidiness.
18. **Open to growth:** Displays the willingness to explore change.

As of this writing, Denise has a new boyfriend who treats her respectfully and accepts her influence. They have been dating exclusively for two months. A couch potato when they met, he honored her request and walks or works out with her every other day. He isn't the most romantic man in the world, nor is he psychologically sophisticated, but he otherwise measures up well against the list of desirable traits. At first, Denise was uncomfortable with him ("I don't know the rules with a nice guy") and wasn't even sure she deserved to be treated so respectfully, but now is beginning to enjoy the benefits of being with a good man. When she jokes about fixing her broken picker, Denise smiles in a genuine way that makes me feel good about being her therapist.

Lastly, there is an old and wise guideline: would this person make a good parent for your children? Or, if this man or woman was your own child, would you be proud of him or her? If not, be wary.

Broken Pickers, Making Repairs Worksheet

Yes, people have the capacity to grow and change, but if your potential mate has too many small issues or one fatal flaw, the relationship is simply not going to work. Here is a worksheet that can serve as a screening tool or a point of discussion if you're considering a committed relationship. Go ahead and grade your potential partner with regard to the traits listed in the last section, that's what your picker is supposed to do.

A=Best
B=Good
C=Fair
D=Poor

1. Emotional stability. _____

_____
_____

2. Good physical health. _____

_____
_____

3. Balanced life. _____

_____
_____

4. Sense of humor. _____

_____
_____

5. Communicates effectively. ____

_____

_____

6. Problem-solving ability. ____

_____

_____

7. Creates a safe space. ____

_____

_____

8. Good friend. ____

_____

_____

9. Maturity. ____

_____

_____

10. Compatible values, goals and priorities. ____

_____

_____

11. Honesty. ____

_____

_____

12. Respectful. ____

_____

_____

13. Romantic. _____

_____

_____

14. Spiritual. _____

_____

_____

15. Sexual compatibility. _____

_____

_____

16. Child rearing. _____

_____

_____

17. Compatible lifestyle. _____

_____

_____

18. Open to growth. _____

_____

_____

Additional Comments: _____

_____

_____

_____

_____

_____

_____

3
The Art Of Collecting Information

Reality is that which, when you stop believing in it, doesn't go away.
—Philip K. Dick

To treat your facts with imagination is one thing, but to imagine your facts is another.
—John Burroughs

Question reality, especially if it contradicts the evidence of your hopes and dreams.
—Robert Brault

One of the most important life skills you can learn is to collect information based on reality. Having this skill can make a difference in regards to having a successful career, a healthy relationship, feeling good about yourself, and meeting your goals and dreams. Being reality-based is essential if you are to make good decisions.

A smart woman has an effective radar system, and she uses the information she obtains from scanning her environment. Operating in reality is the number one way to protect yourself. Only when you're in reality can you make healthy choices, arrive at correct judgments, effectively problem-solve, or step back from a potentially dangerous situation.

Just because you are infatuated or attracted to someone does not mean he or she is a good match for you. Avoid collecting info when you're drinking, drugging, or just had sex. All of the above throw off your radar and have the potential to put you in harm's way. One of the best ways to make a mistake about a new relationship is to jump into bed with someone you've just met. It is like putting on rose-colored glasses and trying to get a clear picture of what is really happening. If you doubt yourself and question whether your information is real, it is best to do reality checks with people you respect and who have your best interests at heart. Don't be afraid to look information up on the Internet, read, go back to school, get counseling, talk to your minister, beam up prayers, and ask for direction.

Be in your Adult when you're collecting information. Pay close attention to inner cues that suggest your Inner Child might be running the show.

When I have the feeling of "energized insistence" I am quite certain it is my Child who wants to be in charge. By that I mean, when I feel impulsive, impatient, overly eager to come to a decision, in too big a hurry, or have too much energy on the issue, then I'm nearly always in my Inner Child. This is the time to wait and see, to summon a more mature and Adult part of my personality to take over. This is the time to slow down and decide to collect more information on the subject.

Here is a useful list to help you develop the ability to collect information based on reality:

1. **Get clear on the issue.** Whether it's choosing a boyfriend, partner, or husband, taking a trip, accepting a job, returning to school, terminating a pregnancy, or carrying one to term. Talk about it, write about it, read about it, meditate on it, pray on it.

2. **Make certain you're in your Inner Adult.** Calm down, center yourself, get support, and take your time to collect the information you need.

3. **Watch for cues that you may be coming from your Inner Child.** Do you feel overly excited, silly, impatient, or energized? Are you suffering from denial, amnesia, or raging hormones?

4. **Attend to your intuition.** Does your choice, judgment, or solution give you a "funny" or uncomfortable feeling in your gut? If so, figure out what your body is trying to tell you. Remember, the only time your intuition doesn't work is when you're not using it.

5. **Be drug and alcohol-free when collecting information.** Sober decisions are not always correct, but they have a much higher chance of being so.

6. **Do not be acting out any addictions or affected by mental health issues when making decisions.** I refer to gambling, spending, computer-obsessed, addictive relationships, manic-depression, etc. Seek help from a counselor and assess taking medication.

7. **Avail yourself to your resources.** Ask for help from friends, family, counselors, ministers, and life coaches. Sit down and read, write, browse the Internet, and attend classes.

8. **Be brutally honest with yourself.** If you find you are hiding information from the people you know, you're more than likely in your Child and about to do something you should not be doing.

9. **Ask yourself,** "Is this going to hurt me or anyone else?"

10. **Stay away from sex when assessing a relationship until you are clear that this level of intimacy is a good idea.** If you are already having sex tell your sexual companion you wish to slow down the pace and stop for now.

11. **Are you lonely?** Don't let this be the reason you are choosing to be in a relationship. The reality is you will settle and then suffer more than the suffering of loneliness.

12. **Be mindful.** Ask God, pray, meditate, exercise, be in nature, journal, seek a source that will help you to be centered and calm when you're gathering information.

13. **Practice supportive self-talk when managing yourself around this issue.** Examples:
    - "I need to wait. I can't gather all this information at once."
    - "Why am I in such a hurry?"
    - "I'm afraid I'm about to do something I'll regret. I have to stop and think this through."
    - "I need to center myself. I can't collect real or reliable information until I do."
    - "Maybe I need a second or third or fourth opinion. For whatever reason, I don't trust myself right now."
    - "I'm feeling so excited and impulsive. This feels like my Child part!"
    - "That funny feeling in my gut tells me something is amiss. I need to slow down and be sure I'm in reality."

This kind of honest and positive self-talk can ground you in reality and ensure that your judgments, decisions, and solutions have a better chance of success. By keeping an eye out for your Inner Child and summoning your Adult to handle these important situations, you will protect yourself from many moments of failure, suffering and potential danger. The marriage of gathering information based on reality and patience makes for good choices and a safer life.

A moment of patience may ward off great disaster.
A moment of impatience may ruin a whole life.

—Chinese proverb

4
What Is A Healthy Person?

Health is not simply the absence of sickness.

—Hannah Green

Sigmund Freud, the founder of psychoanalysis, wrote nearly twenty major works on psychopathology. At the end of his career, a clever interviewer asked the great thinker a provocative question: "You've numerous books on mental illness . . . what is mental health?"

Without hesitation, Freud answered, "The ability to love, work, and play."

I love this answer because it allows us to look at ourselves and quickly assess whether we are living life in balance. Maybe we work too much, maybe we need more loving relationships, maybe we have forgotten how to play and relax - any of these issues could make our lives unfulfilling and unhealthy.

While I believe there is no one official definition of mental health, I would like to expand a bit on Freud's answer. Certainly, it's not enough to say that a healthy person is one who has the absence of a mental disorder. It has to have more to do with values, virtues, talents, coping skills, emotional stability, and the ability to connect with others. Let's consider seven positive characteristics that would make up a healthy person (all apply to both men and women, though I have alternated examples to keep it simple).

1. **Self-acceptance.** She is reasonably comfortable with who she is and both respects and loves herself. Her self-appraisal is realistic in that she sees her faults, but doesn't get stuck in negative thoughts about being unworthy, undeserving, or unlovable. She can understand and deal with her own shortcomings and is open to growth and self-improvement.

2. **Sustaining relationships.** He is capable of meaningful and intimate relationships with friends and significant others. He can hold others in high regard and is not unfairly judgmental or critical. He feels empathy and goodwill toward people in general and is capable of giving love to those with whom he becomes close. He can tolerate vulnerability and ambivalence and love others deeply.

3. **Effective communication.** Able to accurately identify her feelings, she can assert the appropriate need that will satisfy her. For example, she is hurt by the insensitive comment of a total stranger and knows she needs consolation and soothing so she seeks out and gets a hug from a close friend. This returns her to a state of emotional balance. She can communicate her needs in ways that are adult and authentic without resorting to whining, begging, manipulating, or violating the boundaries of others. She is not afraid of defining herself by saying what's so in a way that is open, honest, and direct. You know where she stands. She is a "what you see is what you get" kind of woman.

4. **Morals and values.** He has a good moral compass, makes conscious good choices, and lives his life with purpose and integrity. He is a trustworthy person and also able to make accurate discriminations about who is and who isn't worthy of trust. He shows mature self-control and takes responsibility for his actions, including aggressive and sexual impulses.

5. **Effective coping.** She is able to adapt to the demands of life and to be resilient and resourceful in the face of stress. As such, she can deal with difficult situations through a combination of support from others, prayer, meditation, exercise, and life activities she finds interesting and pleasurable. She has a support system in the community to deal with life's inevitable frustrations. She maintains a positive mental attitude regardless of her circumstances. On those rare occasions that she melts down emotionally, she knows what to

do to pull herself back together. She can face emergencies with patience and perspective.

6. **Emotional regulation.** He is aware of his emotions and able to express them in mature ways that meet his needs while defining who he is. He can regulate his emotions; that is, he can control, direct or communicate them effectively without resorting to alcohol, drugs, eating disorders, sexual addiction, spending or gambling compulsions. His moods are stable. He can be spontaneous and playful without acting-out in ways that could be dangerous or self-defeating.

7. **Meaningful work.** She is able to work productively. If she has chosen to be a homemaker, she uses her multiple skill sets to effectively manage her home and nuture her family. If she chooses to be employed outside the home she is able to strike a healthy balance between work and career. Either way, her work is meaningful to her and in sync with her dreams and goals. She can function from her Adult ego state and assume financial responsibility for herself. She is confident in her abilities and can plan correctly for her future.

Are you a healthy person according to the above seven characteristics? Fill out the expanded 50-item checklist below to see your strengths, and areas of needed improvement. If you meet most of the criteria, congratulations, you are blessed. If you fall short on one or more of the traits, don't beat up on yourself, but get to work on improving the areas in question. You are worth the effort! Note: you can also fill out the checklist for another person such as a boyfriend, husband, friend, boss, etc.

What Is A Healthy Person? Worksheet

This list does not include everything but it is a great tool for screening for a partner or friends. We all have things to work on. This list gives us an idea of where we are on the spectrum and the work we and others need to do.

1. ____ Self-respecting.
2. ____ Feels whole and self-accepting.
3. ____ Respectful of others.
4. ____ Positive self-esteem.
5. ____ Open to growth.
6. ____ Meaningful relationships.
7. ____ Recognizes separateness, but capable of closeness.
8. ____ Not unfairly critical or judgmental.
9. ____ Empathetic.
10. ____ Loving.
11. ____ Asserts needs without whining, manipulating, violating boundaries.
12. ____ Able to spend time alone.
13. ____ Authentic and genuine.
14. ____ Says what's so.
15. ____ Able to relax.
16. ____ Good moral compass.
17. ____ Takes care of self medically.
18. ____ Lives with purpose and integrity.
19. ____ Healthy eating, regular exercise.
20. ____ Takes responsibility for actions.
21. ____ Handles stress.
22. ____ Has a regular sleep schedule.
23. ____ Trustworthy, able to assess trustworthiness of others.

24.____ Not dependent on alcohol or drugs.

25.____ Stable moods.

26.____ No compulsions.

27.____ Good coping skills.

28.____ Peaceful from within.

29.____ Good support system.

30.____ Positive mental attitude.

31.____ Productive worker.

32.____ Open, direct communication.

33.____ Life in balance.

34.____ Listens to other's feelings.

35.____ Responsible financially.

36.____ Can receive guidance.

37.____ Self-confident.

38.____ Learns from mistakes.

39.____ Ability to problem solve.

40.____ Honesty with self and others.

41.____ Expresses feelings in a non-hurtful way.

42.____ Has good boundaries and limits.

43.____ Works towards dreams and goals.

44.____ Forgiving.

45.____ In touch with mystery of life.

46.____ Sustained by religious or spiritual belief system.

47.____ Has a guiding conscience.

48.____ Realizes people are more important than things.

49.____ Practices humility.

50.____ Doesn't make self a victim.

5
Having Healthy Needs Versus Being 'Needy'

One must desire something to be alive.

—Margaret Deland

How helpless we are, like netted birds, when we are caught by desire!

—Belva Plain

We have seen how healthy persons can identify their needs and get them met in order to get back to a state of emotional balance. This whole issue of neediness is confusing to many women as they mistakenly believe there is something wrong with having needs and expressing them. Men have a slightly different version of this confusion: whereas women tend to acknowledge their needs, but don't approve of them, men often try to pretend as if they have no needs in the first place.

Let's get real. We all have needs, it's part of our mammalian nature and what has allowed us to survive as a species. Needs are good—they organize us to get whatever it is that will be satisfying and return our organism to homeostasis. If I am thirsty, I get a drink of water. If I am hungry, I seek food to quell the uncomfortable sensations. If I am lonely, I seek out friends or companions to talk with, eat with, play with, laugh with, and so on. If I am grieving, I release my tears and attempt to get emotional support to ease my suffering.

The confusion arises only when our needs become overwhelming, and we let the Child part of ourselves take over in a desperate attempt to soothe ourselves. Consider the woman who has for whatever reason isolated herself for a year and now discovers she is terribly lonely. If she is in her Adult, she will do whatever is necessary to get some contact, hang out with friends, join a book club or a quilting group, or participate in online dating to meet her need for companionship. However, if she is desperately lonely, in other words "needy," she might be willing to give up her power and lose herself in the first man who shows her any attention. Now she looks to him to make her feel whole. He becomes the barometer for her self-esteem and happiness; that is, if he is being nice to her she feels good about herself and experiences happiness. If he is unkind or pulls away, she dislikes herself and feels unhappy. Because she is in her Child part, she may be willing to whine, pout, manipulate, or beg him to take care of her needs.

My client Becky was "needy" in the pejorative sense I am describing. After not dating for several years, she hooked up with a man she knew from high school after running into him at a reunion. They started dating and became sexually intimate even though he was crystal clear he was not interested in a committed relationship. When he was with her and showing her the attention she so craved, all was well with the world. When he pulled back and ignored her phone calls and text messages, she would fly into a rage and test his boundaries. She did this by "blowing up" his cell phone, "stalking" him on Facebook, showing up unexpectedly at his workplace, and driving by his residence late at night to see if he was with another woman. When she realized she could not get him to commit and that he was really only available for "booty calls," she started overeating to make the bad feelings go away. Now she really hated herself. She convinced herself there was no point in doing anything unless he was with her, and she fell into a deep depression.

Therapy focused on helping Becky relocate the Adult part of her so she could assert her needs as a mature woman. This meant acknowledging the need, but not giving up herself or her power in order to get needs met. It meant keeping an eye on her Child part and not allowing that scared part of her to take over and act out. When she learned how to approach her needs in a healthier way, she stopped feeling "needy" and ended the "booty calls" that robbed her of her self-esteem. Instead of overeating to make the frustration go away, she began meditation and working out at a gym.

NEEDY (Coming from your wounded Inner Child)	GETTING HEALTHY NEEDS MET (Coming from your Inner Adult)
Controlling	Going with flow
Demanding	Clearly requesting
Expecting others to know your feelings, thoughts, and needs	Graciously educating others about your feelings, thoughts, and needs
Impulsive	Thinking it through
Insistent	Flexible, counter-offering
Jealous	Secure
Manipulating	Open and direct
Playing victim or martyr	Honest integrity
Pouting	Expressing feelings and needs appropriately
Stalking	Honoring boundaries
Sulking	Holding emotions
Unreasonable	Reasonable
Violating boundaries	Respectful
Whining	Problem-solving
Withdrawing	Engaged
Yelling	Centered, expressing appropriately

Need is a four-letter word, but there is nothing wrong with having or expressing your needs. It's the way you do it that counts, as evidenced by the list above. We're all needy, it's only when our needs overwhelm us and we slip into our wounded Child part or become desperate and manipulative that we get ourselves in trouble. This is what Buddha taught 2,500 years ago – that we suffer when wholesome desire becomes unwholesome craving. As with Becky, the mind obsesses and clings to a particular outcome.

Be aware of your needs, express them clearly and responsibly and your life will be happier and more fulfilling. If you are sharing your life with people who ignore or disrespect your needs, or with people who either shame you or exploit you because of your needs, a new need emerges; namely, finding new people with whom you can safely share your life. As always, stay in your Adult and drive with your headlights on.

6
Relationships Based On Fear

Fear can be headier than whisky, once man has acquired a taste for it.
—Donald Downes

The suspense is terrible. I hope it will last.

—Oscar Wilde

Immature love says: "I love you because I need you."
Mature love says: "I need you because I love you."

—Erich Fromm

There are many ways we seek an adrenalin rush. Jumping out of perfectly good airplanes, flying them, sailing in a windstorm, racing a motorcycle, mountain climbing, bungee jumping, or skydiving. There must be a joy in these types of risk taking. Calculated or not, the result is the same: some people do it again and again because it's addictive.

So it goes in a relationship. A person gets a "high" in an addictive relationship. It's just like raising your arms on a roller coaster, with the fear of being thrown out of the car or careening out of control. It goes beyond the excitement of being with someone new, this kind of relationship values the "thrill" over safety and security.

Unresolved childhood issues make fear-based relationships look attractive. Being in a relationship with someone who is unstable or even a little dangerous creates an excitement that can override old feelings of abandonment, rejection, and low self-esteem. When the fearsome person you're "in love" with pays attention to you, life is good. He or she represents the parental figure that wounded you or didn't give you what you needed as a child. Anyone who has been in one will tell you, you can literally get a "high" or a "rush" off a fear-based relationship.

Many people who are addicted in a relationship will say: "This is the best sex I've ever had," or "I can't get him out of my head!" They find themselves obsessively analyzing the relationship and feel overwhelmed by strong feelings of emptiness and longing. (Have your friends or family ever said they are "burned out" on listening to your obsessing?) Do not confuse this kind of relationship with healthy love, which leaves you feeling calm, centered, and whole. In a healthy relationship, we like the way we feel about ourselves when we are with the person we love. In a fear-based one, we often find ourselves feeling insecure, inadequate, and little.

Fear-based relationships leave you feeling like a vulnerable child, scrambling for love and attention and depressed when you can't get it. This kind of relationship can cause us to lose our self-esteem, time, energy, and focus. By giving away our power, it will also rob us of our dreams and goals. If you find yourself in serial fear-based relationships, or one long one, strongly consider seeking professional help. Extricating yourself on your own is nearly impossible.

Relationships Based On Fear Worksheet

Carefully reflect on these questions below, stay out of denial, and use your answers to screen who you are spending time with. Look at who you become when you are around these people. Be aware of the time you spend being anxious or fearful, or feeling that you've lost your perspective or yourself.

1. How do I feel about myself in this relationship?

_____

_____

_____

2. Do I feel like I am scrambling for love and attention?

_____

_____

_____

3. Do I feel depressed being in this relationship?

_____

_____

_____

4. Have I lost my self-esteem?

_____

_____

_____

5. Have I lost my time, energy, and focus on my personal dreams and goals?

_____

_____

_____

6. What are my personal dreams and goals?

_____

_____

_____

7. Has my wholesome desire turned into thrill-based craving?

_____

_____

_____

8. How can I best Turn, Shift, and Focus Back on to what my dreams and goals are now?

_____

_____

_____

7
Open To Growth Versus Giving In To Fear

Patterning your life around other's opinions is nothing more than slavery.
—Lawana Blackwell

If two men agree on everything, you may be sure that one of them is doing the thinking.

—Lyndon B. Johnson

When looking for a friend or partner, screen for someone who is open to growth and make yourself open to growth, as well. This is not to be confused with someone who goes along with everything because they are afraid to take a stand. The difference is that someone open to growth has a moral compass, a value system, and a strong sense of self. By strong sense of self I mean a person who defines a self by expressing freely their needs, desires, feelings, and opinions.

Pleasing others, usually based on the fear of abandonment, drives the person who does not assert herself. If I express myself and displease others, they won't like me and will choose not to be my friend/lover/spouse/ fill in the blank. A person who habitually gives in to fear "goes the way of the wind," changing colors like a human chameleon. Rather than risk being seen for who they really are, they try to mold themselves to what they believe others want and lose themselves in the process. This is a prescription for resentment, low self-esteem, and continued insecurity.

Donna grew up in an alcoholic family system and learned to squelch her own needs so as to avoid the disappointment and frustration she felt when she tried expressing herself. She just gave up, rarely expressing her true feelings until this became part of her character. As an adult, she never asserted her needs or declined any request and described herself as having "no backbone." In therapy, Donna learned that her false self guaranteed more frustration and agreed to try out doing something different. An opportunity occurred when a ne'er-do-well friend asked if he could borrow Donna's car.

Just as Donna was about to comply, she remembered her homework and screwed up the courage to say no. "I'd loaned this guy my car in the past and he always returned it without replacing the gas and this was just not okay!"

The friend acted huffy when Donna refused, but didn't end the relationship, and Donna was justifiably proud of her new behavior. Had she loaned the car, she would have resented the friend and strained the relationship anyway.

Donna made the healthy choice, showing she was open to growth and willing to take a risk. By declining her friend's request, Donna defined a self and gained self-esteem by acting on her true feelings. When we are open to growth we can learn from past mistakes and go forward, creating a future focus rather than being stuck in a past pattern that doesn't work.

Take a risk. Express your true self and see if you don't gain in self-esteem, even if it creates a temporary feeling of discomfort. Donna opened herself to improving her assertive skills and felt like she had a new lease on life.

Open To Growth Versus Giving In To Fear Worksheet

List three areas of your life where you would like to grow and improve yourself. Hint: identify a desire or need you regularly fail to express; something you are afraid to say, but needs to be said; or a difference of opinion you normally keep to yourself. Dig deep!

1. _____
_____
_____
_____

2. _____
_____
_____
_____

3. _____
_____
_____
_____

8
The 'Near Miss' Relationship

Near miss relationships suffer from a fatal flaw. The challenge is to recognize that what is wrong cannot be fixed and find the courage to leave.
—S. Lee Nye, Ph.D.

Never try to teach a pig to sing. It never works, and it just pisses off the pig!
—Anonymous

Some relationships seem wonderful, especially in those magical first weeks and months of infatuation while you still idealize one another. Things are going well and your new partner may have many good qualities. Then an issue emerges and an important part of the relationship no longer works for you. Maybe he drinks a little too much on the weekend, tries to boss you around when he's stressed out, or responds unsupportively when you share your most vulnerable feelings. Most of the time you like him, but you are beginning to like yourself less when you're with him. You realize the "dance" you do with him doesn't feel quite right, the way you relate as a couple feels off.

My friend Lee Nye calls this a 'near miss,' an otherwise functional relationship that is compromised by problems of character. You try to address the issue and make your feelings known, but he still doesn't get it. Maybe you tell him exactly what you want and go out of your way to avoid sounding critical, but he still doesn't come through. Apply enough pressure and he might promise to change the behavior that upsets you, but it never really happens. Why? Because the problem is a part of his character, and his typical ways of thinking and relating just don't work in a loving, committed relationship. Some men can accept our influence and some lack the strength and maturity. The "near miss" man is the one who has a fatal flaw that prevents him from connecting intimately with a woman.

I am reminded of the tale of the scorpion and the frog, a lesson that can save you from a 'near miss' relationship and therefore from a lot of heartache. I've heard several versions, but this is my favorite.

A flash flood traps a scorpion on an island in the middle of a raging river. The water continues to rise, and he will soon drown unless rescued. He calls to a nearby frog and asks if he can climb on his back for a ride to safety.

"What . . . do you think I am crazy?" the frog says. "I know who you are. You're a scorpion. If I let you on my back, you'll sting me and I'll drown."

"Think it over," the scorpion replies. "I can't swim. If I sting you, then I'll sink in the water and I'll drown too. You'll be rescuing me, saving a life. I promise I won't sting you."

Feeling sympathetic and taking him at his word, the frog allows the scorpion to scuttle onto his back.

Halfway across the river, the scorpion stings the frog. With his dying breath, the frog gasps, "Why would you do that? Now I'm going to die and you're going to drown in the river."

"I don't know," the scorpion answers. "I guess it's just my nature. After all, I am a scorpion."

Rita was thinking of marrying a man with whom she had a lot of fun, but who sometimes controlled her with indirect threats of violence. "He's never actually hit me," she rationalized. "He just screams at me and gives me this really scary look. The rest of the time he's really nice."

We devised a kind of litmus test to give this man an opportunity to either heal the relationship or expose his fatal flaw. Rita was coached to tell him how she felt when he threatened her and also to make a specific request of what she wanted. She told him it terrified her to see his rage and asked that he take an anger management class at a nearby counseling center. She told him she'd lost respect for him and wouldn't even consider marrying him unless he completed the class and demonstrated a sincere willingness to change. She also told him she wanted to feel safe with him and that they would have a chance if he would own up to the problem and get a handle on his anger. He agreed to take the class, but never signed up, always having some excuse or another for why he didn't have the time.

Rita had dodged the proverbial bullet. By expressing how her boyfriend's behavior made her feel and asking directly for what she wanted, she gave him an opportunity to accept her influence and make the desired changes. His response was to dismiss her feelings and needs because he wasn't at all interested in improving himself. In a sense, he showed his scorpion nature, as if he was who he was and would not change. Men who use anger to manipulate and control their women don't like to give it up. Such control is based on insecurity.

Had Rita chosen to stay in this 'near miss' relationship, she would have eventually lost her valuable time, her positive energy, and her true self. By putting him to the test, she realized the "potential" she saw in this man was not going to materialize. That gave her all she needed to know to move on. Indeed, she missed the good times with him and the hope for a future together, but in the long run she saved herself a ton of grief and quite possibly her safety.

9
How To Spot A Manipulator

Without feelings of respect, what is there to distinguish men from beasts?!
—Confucius

When screening for healthy, safe people, notice whether or not they use manipulation. A manipulator is someone who influences or controls your opinions, decisions and/or behavior by using tricky or unscrupulous means. For example, "If I pout or withdraw, or yell, I can get you to have sex with me even when you don't want to."

Here are the thirty most common ways you can be manipulated (notice the subtle differences). Always keep in mind manipulation is a game that takes two to play. You can choose not to participate. If the person in question amasses more than three checkmarks, you need to seriously question whether you want them in your world!

_____1. **Blaming (you or others).**

_____2. **Caretaking or rescuing (to keep you from claiming power).**

_____3. **Controlling (you or others).**

_____4. **Crazymaking (denial of reality causing you to question your perceptions).**

_____5. **Creating crisis or chaos (distractions to avoid responsibility).**

_____6. **Criticizing (you or others).**

_____7. **Debating (to wear you down, "double talk" to confuse the issue).**

_____8. **Distorting reality (to achieve a hidden agenda).**

_____9. **Distracting (to change the issue).**

_____10. **Dramatizing (to make your feelings less valid).**

_____11. **Exploding (controlling through fear).**

____12. **Guilt-tripping (inducing guilt to maneuver you).**

____13. **Ingratiation (making you feel obligated, "you owe me").**

____14. **Invalidating (you or others).**

____15. **Judging (you or others).**

____16. **Lip service or patronizing (insincerity to maneuver you).**

____17. **Lying or making false promises (any kind).**

____18. **Making excuses (to avoid responsibility).**

____19. **Mind reading (to avoid listening).**

____20. **Minimizing (to deny impact, cause self-doubt).**

____21. **Placating (pacifying to get you to drop your point of view).**

____22. **Playing helpless (to avoid responsibility).**

____23. **Psychoanalyzing (armchair psychiatry to get the upper hand).**

____24. **Rewriting history (tampering with reality).**

____25. **Shaming (you or others).**

____26. **Silent treatment or shunning (to punish you for being you).**

____27. **Stereotyping or labeling (to reduce you as a person, keep you powerless).**

____28. **Threatening (controlling through fear).**

____29. **Verbally abusing (name calling, put downs, making unfair comparisons).**

____30. **Withholding (emotions, affection, attention or information).**

This is a long list. Be careful, there are a lot of emotional manipulators out there.

10
Damaging Defenses

As a person becomes more and more defensive, he becomes less and less able to perceive accurately the motives, values, and emotions of the sender.

—Jack Gibb

What does it mean to be defensive? Usually it means we're trying to protect ourselves from what we perceive to be another person's complaint, judgment, criticism, or aggression. Is this a bad thing? Of course not. Suppose an emotionally unstable neighbor accuses you of sugaring his gas tank and calls you a "liar" when you deny it. Under such circumstances, it's completely healthy and even necessary to defend your reputation, otherwise you will invite retribution or police action. Unless it would put you in physical danger, it would be improper *not* to defend yourself at a time you're being attacked in an unfair or threatening way.

On the other hand, if we become automatically or chronically defensive at the first sign of criticism, we can't help but damage our relationships. Some people reflexively hit the "defend at all costs" button because they don't want to be held accountable. To admit a shortcoming or wrongdoing would be too much for a fragile ego, so they try to shift responsibility to someone else—usually the person they're arguing with.

Let's say you have a bad habit of interrupting people and your new boyfriend calls you on it. If you reply with, "You do it, too!" you're being overly defensive and not allowing the relationship to heal. The new boyfriend feels "not heard" and invalidated, and you can almost guarantee his emotional temperature will go up, resulting in even more frustration and disappointment. As the communication breaks down, an important precedent has been set for the relationship. Much better is to own your own bad habit and vow to change. Then, do it.

People who become automatically defensive don't want to feel bad about themselves ("I'm acting like a jerk!") or they don't want to experience uncomfortable sensations in their body ("If I'm wrong I will get that shrinking sensation I can't stand!"). So, they refuse to own up to something they may have done or not done, or they won't acknowledge an actual thought or feeling they're having, and this is ruinous to the relationship at hand.

Phil has a gambling addiction and 'lost' his and Dana's life savings of fifty thousand dollars. He agreed to never gamble again, but didn't deal with the real problem; namely, he couldn't regulate his emotions without the distraction of a slot machine that would take him on a dopamine-fueled thrill ride. It didn't matter if he lost money, he couldn't stop himself. When confronted for breaking his promise to Dana and resuming gambling, he said, "It's because you never give me any spending money." With this attempt to shift responsibility, he conveniently forgot that he never had any spending money because he would gamble it away, and the couple would be unable to pay the rent or feed their children. Phil's rigid defensiveness not only precluded his getting real help, but also alienated his enraged wife.

This is an example of a damaging defense. It doesn't allow for effective communication when something is already going wrong. It's like a double whammy. There's a problem (Phil's gambling and deceit), but his defensiveness means they can't discuss it and make corrections (treatment for the problem, making amends, rebuilding trust).

Damaging Defenses Worksheet

Take a look at the following checklist and see if you are relying too much on any of these defenses:

_____1. Anger, attacking, aggression.
_____2. Blaming, shaming, accusing.
_____3. Changing the subject.
_____4. Evading, dodging, avoiding.
_____5. Explaining or over-explaining.
_____6. Complying, placating.
_____7. Debating, arguing without cause.
_____8. Demanding respect or obedience.
_____9. Denying, minimizing.
_____10. Withdrawing.
_____11. Giving the silent treatment.
_____12. Shouting, intimidating, raging.
_____13. Making or implying threats.
_____14. Resorting to profanity.
_____15. Overgeneralizing.
_____16. Grinning, laughing inappropriately.
_____17. Sarcasm, put-downs.
_____18. Quibbling, equivocating.
_____19. Intellectualizing.
_____20. Projecting.
_____21. Deflecting.
_____22. Judging, moralizing, criticizing.
_____23. Justifying.
_____24. Labeling.
_____25. Lying.
_____26. Acting smug or superior.

_____27. Quoting scripture.
_____28. Rationalizing.
_____29. Procrastination, dawdling.
_____30. Tuning out.

There are also personal strategies that are used in support of damaging defenses. These include addictive and other unhealthy behaviors that support avoidance. Give yourself a checkmark if you take care of your needs and regulate your feelings by excessively resorting to the following. Be honest.

_____1. Alcohol.
_____2. Computers.
_____3. Drugs.
_____4. Exercise.
_____5. Fantasy.
_____6. Food.
_____7. Gambling.
_____8. Money.
_____9. People.
_____10. Power.
_____11. Rescuing (pets, projects or people).
_____12. Religiosity (flaunting your religion).
_____13. Sex.
_____14. Spending.
_____15. Tobacco.
_____16. TV.
_____17. Video games.
_____18. Work.

If you see yourself being overly defensive or relying on the above list of addictive avoidance behaviors, here are a few general guidelines:

1. **Acknowledge you have a problem.** In the heat of the moment you might say, "I'm feeling pretty defensive, and I'm afraid I didn't really hear you. Would you mind repeating your point?"

2. **Take a time out to collect your thoughts and gather your resources.**

3. **Watch your experience.** Is there self-talk that's in the way ("This is exactly like when my Mom called me stupid for not knowing how to tell time.")? Are images from the past emerging that you can't tolerate ("If I admit I broke the vase, will I get slapped in the face?")? Are shame feelings being triggered that are just too painful ("If I acknowledge I screwed up the assignment, everyone is going to make fun of me.")?

4. **Look for the root of your problem.** If you can't own up to a fault, is it because you would feel lack of self-esteem and hate yourself, or because it would re-create an old family-of-origin issue that always led to abuse? Or something else?

5. **Commit to change.** Tell yourself you don't have to be perfect, that it's okay to make mistakes and own up to them. It is in your own best interest to drop the damaging defenses and take responsibility. The world will not come to an end.

11
Don't Lose Yourself In The 'Theys'

But it's all right now, I learned my lesson well. You see, ya can't please everyone, so ya got to please yourself.

—Ricky Nelson

There comes a time in life, when you walk away from all the drama and people who created it. Surround yourself with people who make you laugh, forget the bad, and focus on the good. Love the people who treat you right. Pray for the ones who don't. Life is too short to be anything but happy. Falling down is part of life. Getting back up is living.

—Unknown

In 1952, when I was a young girl, eleven-year-old Ricky Nelson joined "The Adventures of Ozzie and Harriet," his parents' family-friendly television sitcom. Within five years Ricky became a teenage heartthrob and rock 'n' roll star, with a number of big hits. His star faded in the mid-sixties, but in 1971 he was invited to play in a reunion show at Madison Square Garden. By this time Ricky had crossed over to country rock and when he tried to play his new material, he was virtually booed off the stage. Shaken, he wrote a song about this experience and, ironically, it became his biggest hit – "Garden Party." The chorus is the topic of this chapter ("But it's all right now, I learned my lesson well. You see, ya can't please everyone, so ya got to please yourself"). Ricky's lesson was that he learned to be true to himself and not lose himself in the 'theys.'

Many of us are afraid to do what we really want to do for fear of what the 'theys' might think or of what they might say to us or about us. We abandon our dreams for fear of being judged, as if someone else has all the answers or knows what's best for us. Consider: Linda wanted to open an espresso stand in the parking lot of a large grocery store. There were no espresso stands within a mile in Linda's coffee-obsessed area of the Pacific Northwest. She negotiated a favorable lease with the grocery store and began looking into what kind of franchise would be most profitable. But then she lost herself in the 'theys.' Her banker and even her husband told her it would be financial suicide to try to start a business when she had no business experience. Linda began do doubt herself, gave up the idea and settled into a deep depression. A few months later, an espresso stand opened in "her" exact location and was wildly successful.

Who are the 'theys' anyway? They could be just about anybody – a controlling spouse, an internalized parent, a real-life parent, your best friend, the next-door neighbor, a self-righteous minister, an audience, or people in general. Keep in mind we define our identities by acknowledging and expressing our true feelings, needs, desires, and opinions. People carve out an identity when they make statements like "I'm joining an antiwar group," or "I've decided to go back to college," or "I want to write a book." When we abandon such dreams because others might disapprove or argue against us, we lose ourselves in the 'theys.' We, in effect, give away our power, abandon our true self, and settle for a false one.

An old story makes the point. An elderly grandfather sets out with his young grandson to go to the market. With them is the old man's donkey. Grandfather places the boy on the donkey's back and off they go. Soon, they pass travelers headed in the opposite direction. One looks over and comments, in a derisive tone, "Will you look at that. That thoughtless boy makes the old man walk on a hot day!" Grandfather and grandson hear the comment and decide it would be best to trade places. They continue on and soon they encounter more travelers. This time they hear the comment, "Will you look at that. That thoughtless old man makes the little boy walk on a hot day!" Bewildered, they decide to both walk and avoid any further criticism. Soon, another traveler looks over and says, "Will you look at that. A perfectly good beast of burden and neither of them have the good sense to ride it on a hot day!" Again they stop and this time they decide to both ride the donkey. It isn't long before they pass more travelers and sure enough, one comments, "Will you look at that. How inconsiderate of them to both ride that animal on such a hot day!" Get the point? If you're invested in pleasing the 'theys,' you will never get it right.

There's nothing wrong with wanting or even seeking approval, but when it means selling yourself down the river, you've lost yourself in the 'theys.' This doesn't mean you can't listen to feedback from others or factor others' ideas into your decision-making. But in the end, you must learn to follow your own heart to be truly you. The truth is most people are so busy and focused on their own lives that they aren't paying real attention to what you are doing, anyway. The visionaries of the world have introduced change precisely because they were willing to follow their dreams and tune out the naysayer 'theys.' Be a visionary, or at least be yourself.

Let yourself be silently drawn by the strange pull of what you really love. It will not lead you astray.

—Rumi

DO IT ANYWAY

People are often unreasonable, illogical, and self centered;
Forgive them anyway.

If you are kind, people may accuse you of selfish, ulterior motives;
Be kind anyway.

If you are successful you will win some false friends and true enemies;
Succeed anyway.

If you are honest and frank, people may cheat you;
Be honest and frank anyway.

What you spend years building, someone could destroy overnight;
Build anyway.

If you find serenity and happiness, they may be jealous;
Be happy anyway.

The good you do today, people will often forget tomorrow;
Do good anyway.

Give the world the best you have, and it may never be enough;
Give the world the best you've got anyway.

You see, in the final analysis, it is between you and God;
It was never between you and them anyway.

—Mother Theresa

Don't Lose Yourself In The 'Theys' Worksheet

If we are always guided by other people's thoughts, what is the point of having our own?

—Anonymous

Pay attention to your thoughts and catch yourself worrying about the disapproving 'theys.' If you're tempted to negate yourself for fear of what someone else might think or say, consider the moment as an opportunity for self-actualization and personal growth. Then, focus in on your situation and notice how giving away your power feels in your body. Do you feel anxious or fearful? Do you experience a tight or uncomfortable sensation in your chest or gut? Be aware that you're wrestling with the 'theys' and make a commitment to be true to yourself. Face the fear no matter how scary or unfamiliar it feels to hold your ground. Support yourself with some positive self-talk along the lines of, "I'm a grownup. I refuse to give my power to anyone else." Or, have a chuckle and remember Ricky's lyrics: "You see, ya can't please everyone, so ya got to please yourself."

Practice by listing some situations where you are worried about what others will think of you, then keep track of bodily/emotional cues that inform you you're about to make a mistake. Finally, write out the appropriate self-talk that will ensure you don't lose yourself in the 'theys.'

Situation	**Emotional/Bodily Cues**	**Self-Talk**
1. _____	_____	_____
		_____
		_____
2. _____	_____	_____
		_____
		_____
3. _____	_____	_____
		_____
		_____
4. _____	_____	_____
		_____
		_____
5. _____	_____	_____
		_____
		_____
6. _____	_____	_____
		_____
		_____
7. _____	_____	_____
		_____
		_____
8. _____	_____	_____
		_____
		_____
9. _____	_____	_____
		_____
		_____
10. _____	_____	_____
		_____
		_____

12
Independence And Intimacy Can Co-Exist

With rare exceptions, how couples deal with differences is far more important than what the differences actually are.

—Robert W. Resnick, Ph.D.

To be independent is essentially to be free from the control of others and therefore self-governing. To be intimate is to engage in a close, connected, and authentic relationship. Some people believe that independence and intimacy are incompatible, but they are not.

In order for independence and intimacy to co-exist, each person in the relationship must be committed to open and honest communication, and each must set healthy boundaries to define what they think, feel, and stand for. This doesn't mean one person cannot influence the other and, in fact, the marital guru John Gottman has demonstrated through research how important it is to accept influence from a partner. The trick is to accept influence without losing one's self.

When I was trained to do couples therapy, counselors were encouraged to explore the couple's conflicts around money, sex, in-laws, and children. It turns out that according to the Gottman studies, none of these issues predict whether the couple will be happy or if they'll stay married for a long time. You could have great sex in a lousy marriage or disagree about child-rearing in a good marriage. Rather, it was the influence issue that predicted marital success, particularly, whether the male accepts influence from the female.

Now the other factors become more understandable. To reiterate from the *Broken Pickers* chapter, if the wife tells the husband we can't afford a new 3-D television set, but he comes home with one in the back of the truck, trouble is brewing because he didn't accept influence. Or, if he wants sex every other day and she only wants it once a week and he won't relent, there's an influence problem. To be both independent and intimate (in the latter example), would be for the wife to set her limits and/or compromise and for the husband to authentically share his need, frustration, and disappointment (but not criticize, pout, or manipulate). This is essentially the difference between good conflict and bad conflict.

The only time this will not work is if you don't honestly communicate your needs, fail to set boundaries in a healthy way, or the other person does not honor them. One of the hallmarks of a healthy relationship is to accept and tolerate differences. Let's say the husband is a political conservative and the wife a liberal. If they argue, try to recruit one another to their side, or try to make the other wrong, there will be endless discord. An alternative is to be curious about the points of difference, even if you disagree ("Okay, so you also believe everyone in America should have health insurance, but I consider the cost to be too high."). To accept difference here is to say, "I see it differently," and for this to be okay because independence is celebrated and intimacy is a shared goal.

There's no need to be joined at the hip with our partners or see everything the same way. Having individual interests in a relationship can bring excitement, growth, and respect into a healthy partnership. The key is to strike the right balance between separateness and togetherness, between independence and intimacy. You don't have to give up the things you want to do if you commit to an intimate relationship. You need only identify what you want and define yourself clearly to the significant other. If, instead, you give up what you want and always accommodate to the other or try to erase differences with the other, you will end up frustrated and resentful. Why not be yourself, show up authentically and celebrate differences? Please see the following worksheet to give an idea as to how to divide up your week doing things together and separately.

Independence And Intimacy Can Co-Exist Worksheet

Weekly time sheet for interests and activities.

Weekly Schedule	Individual time	Couple time	Family time
Examples	Golf with friends	Dinner date	Park with kids
	Seminar	Movie	Movie
Monday			
Morning			
Afternoon			
Evening			
Tuesday			
Morning			
Afternoon			
Evening			
Wednesday			
Morning			
Afternoon			
Evening			
Thursday			
Morning			
Afternoon			
Evening			

Friday			
Morning			
Afternoon			
Evening			
Saturday			
Morning			
Afternoon			
Evening			
Sunday			
Morning			
Afternoon			
Evening			

Comments: _____

_____

_____

_____

_____

13
The Blending Of The Inner Adult, Parent, And Child

Grown-ups never understand anything for themselves, and it is tiresome for children to be always and forever explaining things to them.

—Antoine de Saint-Exupery

No matter how "together" we would like to believe we are, we all have "islands of immaturity." These islands can be large or small, depending on the size of the gap between our chronological age and developmental age. Because parts of our personalities have not fully matured and integrated, we are susceptible to wild swings of emotion, we think in irrational ways that cause suffering in our relationships, we endure painful symptoms of depression and anxiety, and we get stuck in telling ourselves stories that virtually guarantee unhappiness.

A client, an attractive and intelligent woman in her mid-forties, recently told me, "I know he cheated on me and then lied about it. All my friends tell me I should dump him, and I know they're right, but I just can't. I can't bear to be without him."

It was our first session, and I resisted the temptation to give her advice—to loan her my Adult, since hers was so obviously off duty. Her words came from a dependent and insecure Little Girl part that was willing to put up with bad boyfriend behavior in order to avoid feeling alone and frightened. This is a good example of a woman not acting as a whole and not integrated in a way that allowed for mature judgment and action. She was essentially immobilized by fear that came from an Inner Child part that never got what she needed. When we mature properly as a result of good parenting we enter adulthood with a sense of secure attachment, strong separation, integrated parts, and personal power. My client's Child was on duty at a time when she desperately needed her Adult or Parent part in control. I knew that in time she would listen to her own inner wisdom, but for now there was work to do that would help her to grow up.

On one of my visits to China I was fortunate enough to be asked to address a medical school in Beijing. In particular, the mental health department wanted me to speak on the issue of western psychology and what we considered to be healthy coping skills. After a generous and some-what lofty introduction, I walked to the podium and looked out at a sea of white coats, hats, and expectant faces. My translator had just taken a place next to me when I felt my body begin to shake with anxiety. I took a giant gulp and noticed how my heart hammered against my chest. What was I going to say? How would I be received? What if I made a mistake and said something ignorant? What if the audience or someone in the audience attacked what I had to say?

Instantly, I recognized this voice as that of my Inner Child and the feelings of inadequacy as emanating from my childhood. Having been in this state before, I knew precisely what to do. I took a deep breath and informed my Child part she had no business dealing with a situation such as this and visualized her in a safe place back in the hotel room. Next, I summoned the most mature, professional and Adult part of me and began the presentation. My Adult knows how to cope with this kind of stress and knows the subject material. My speech went beautifully, but only because the grown-up part of me delivered it. The doctors invited me to come back.

We all have in us the parts of the Inner Adult, Parent and Child. We couldn't get rid of the Child part even if we wanted to (and we shouldn't - note Saint-Exupery's famous quote under the chapter heading), so it benefits us to get a Parent or Adult part to take care of the Child. When the different parts communicate well with one another we function at a higher level; namely, we have a healthier self, we cope better, and we enjoy more satisfy-ing relationships. Knowing the basic qualities of our various inner parts helps us to know our capabilities and limitations, as well as consciously being in the right part to succeed at life. In other words, choosing the right time and place to be in our Child, Parent, or Adult will allow you to remedy any deficits in maturity. Take a few minutes and study the common descriptions below:

Adult	**Parent**	**Child (Healthy)**
Rational	Nurturing	Vulnerable
Logical	Empathetic	Enthusiastic
Grounded in reality	Listens	Playful, Artistic
Mature in thinking	Sets limits	Self-focused
Mature in judgment	Knows limits	Immature
Mature in actions	Guides and structures	Impulsive
Takes time to respond	Patient	Reactive, impatient
Appropriate Actions	Appropriate response	Inappropriate at times
Grown up	Gentle, encourages	Fearful, oversensitive
Resourceful	Supports, calm	Overwhelmed
Problem solving	Provides place to solve	Creative
Connected to outer world	Provides safety	Center of world
Discriminating	Not Critical	Impressionable, naïve
Asserts needs	Attends to basic needs	May suppress needs
Makes requests	Attends to desires	Demanding
Moderates desires	Acknowledges desires	May be ruled by desires
Expresses feelings	Acknowledges feelings	Unskilled with feelings
Sets limits	Knows limits	Tests limits
Spiritual, religious	Wise	Playful, joyful, creative

There are many more examples. These are just a few. We will have more possibility of fulfilling our dreams and goals if we know who is in the driver's seat.

We're all made up of a collection of personality parts that are very much like the archetypes. Archetypes, according to the brilliant psycho-analyst Carl Jung, are original models of personality we all share in a collective unconscious. Simply put, they influence how we think and act and relate. Here is a list of parts many, if not all of us, possess: the Adult, Parent, Child, Great Mother, Wise Old Woman, Sage Old Man, Hero, Innocent, Villain, Damsel in Distress, Witch, Underdog, Trickster, Saboteur, and so on. As you might imagine, if you are acting in accord with one of your archetypes or personality parts, *and don't know it,* you are in for a world of painful confusion.

To illustrate, suppose your boyfriend of six weeks asks you to go on a three-week Mediterranean cruise. You haven't yet slept with him and the distrustful part of you suspects this is his way of bedding you. Outside of conscious awareness, you slip into your saboteur. Now, instead of operating from your Adult and checking out your assumption and setting some boundaries for what could be the vacation of a lifetime, you flip into your saboteur (yes, we all have one). The saboteur begins to find fault with every little thing about him, however minute, that could possibly bother you. Now, without even knowing how you did it, you can in all probability kiss the cruise and the new boyfriend goodbye.

Obviously, it benefits us to know when one of our personality parts has taken over so we can take appropriate measures. It reminds me of the old Abbott and Costello baseball skit, "Who's on First?" (a YouTube must if you haven't heard it). In this, the legendary duo's signature routine, there's a total communication breakdown as Costello tries to learn the names of players on a baseball team. When he says "Who's on first?" Abbott replies, "Yes" (because the first baseman's name happens to be Who). It goes downhill from there, and that's also what happens if you think you're in your part when you're really in your child or any other part. Hence, if you don't know who's on first, you cannot possibly manage your life in a mature and effective way.

14
The Adult

Adulthood is the ever-shrinking period between childhood and old age. It is the apparent aim of modern industrial societies to reduce this period to a minimum.

—Thomas Szasz

Being an adult means accepting those situations where no action is possible.
—John D. MacDonald

What does it mean to be Adult? Certainly it's not based on chronological age, we have too many "children" masquerading as grown-ups to accept that definition. Rather, it's based on being fully mature emotionally and fully developed in terms of personal character.

Borrowing from Transactional Analysis, the Adult is the part of us that receives information from the Parent and Child ego states to analyze, solve problems and successfully navigate the world. Let's take a stab at twenty defining attributes of adulthood:

1. **Able to regulate moods and emotions.**
2. **Separates from family-of-origin, so free from their expectations.**
3. **Transfers primary loyalty from family-of-origin to family-of-procreation.**
4. **Capable of loving others deeply and engaging in intimate relationships.**
5. **Sufficient self-esteem and self-confidence to deal with inevitable setbacks.**
6. **Calms and soothes the Inner Child.**

7. Takes guidance from and negotiates with the Parent part of personality.
8. Rational and logical in decision making; able to think before acting.
9. Values people and relationships.
10. Able to listen to others' feelings and perceptions and accept differences.
11. Understands effective communication is key in healthy relationships.
12. Differentiates between needs and wants, able to delay gratification.
13. Able to learn from mistakes without undue self-criticism.
14. Aware of personal issues and motivated to improve.
15. Remains patient in the face of frustration, flexible confronting obstacles.
16. Sees the world in shades of gray rather than black or white.
17. Takes responsibility for actions; is accountable when out of line.
18. Can cope with stress without falling apart or lapsing into crisis.
19. Handles life's difficulties without resorting to addictive behaviors.
20. Learns to accept that which cannot be changed. Operates in reality.

And, one to grow on: Practices healthy self-care in terms of conscious eating and regular exercise.

Let's look at how this might appear in real life as the Adult in us deals with different and competing parts of the personality.

Example One:

A: (Inner Child to Adult) "I've been working my tail off, and I deserve to go to Hawaii with my friends. I plan to put it on the credit card."

B: (Adult to Inner Child) "We'd better skip the vacation this year because the bank account is down to nothing. Let's do a better job of saving up so we can go next year."

Example Two:

A: (Saboteur to Adult) "I say we're done with Brad. He's not exciting at all and besides, he only makes $50,000 a year!"

B: (Adult to Saboteur) "I get it that Brad's not as exciting as the bad boys we've dated in the past. But he's respectful, dependable and fun when we take charge of what we're doing. I'll try to kick up the excitement level, but we're not going to dump him."

Example Three:

A: (Damsel in Distress to Adult) "I can't pay my student loan and my car payment in the same month. I'm thinking we should ask my parents for help."

B: (Adult to Damsel in Distress) "No, we made a mistake by purchasing a new car when the old one was just fine. Now we need to look at the budget and either tighten our belts or get out from under that big monthly car payment."

Note how there is often a motivated part of us (Adult) that seeks a positive change, and a resistant part (Child) that opposes change. An example would be, "I'm going to lose some weight by cutting down on desserts." (Adult), and "I'm not giving up ice cream, and you can't make me!" (Child). If the Child wins, you lose. It's a choice to stay in your Adult.

15
The Nurturing Parent

Feelings of worth can flourish only in an atmosphere where individual differences are appreciated, mistakes are tolerated, communication is open, and rules are flexible—the kind of atmosphere that is found in a nurturing family.

—Virginia Satir

The trouble with learning to parent on the job is that your child is the teacher.
—Robert Brault

In order to cultivate your Nurturing Parent part, which is essentially a subpersonality within you, you must fully understand what a nurturing parent does for her real-life child.

Is there a more important job than parenting a child? If there is, I don't know what it would be. The impact of your parenting practices will affect your children for the entirety of their lives and may even be passed along to your children's children. To be a nurturing parent you must provide experiences that nourish and educate your children over time. Being a nurturing parent is so much more than nursing or feeding, changing their dirty diapers, bathing them, holding and soothing them, playing with them, reading them bedtime stories, teaching them right from wrong or getting them ready to be responsible and caring citizens. It's about doing all these things and more in a way that says, "You are lovable, you deserve to be protected, you deserve to be happy!"

This will require a great deal of energy, effort, and intention with the goal of helping your child feel safe, secure, and loved unconditionally. Other goals include providing attention and warmth, role-modeling emotional competence and social skills, and showing you are "tuned in" to their needs. Most of all, children need quality time with us, but they also need to know they are loved even when they mess up and make a mistake or do something "stupid."

Nurturing parents provide a watchful eye and guidance and protection for their children as they begin to explore their environment. As they explore and grow, kids need effective praise and not flattery; for example, it works better to say, "You put a lot of time and effort into learning your ABCs today, and I'm proud of you," rather than, "You're awesome!" When nurturing parents use discipline, they use nonphysical and nonviolent means to teach and correct their child's unacceptable behavior. The consequences they hand out make sense and fit the child's age and developmental level.

The Nurturing Parent of your Inner Child is no different than the one that hopefully did all this for her children. If you haven't had your own children, you have ideally internalized a Nurturing Parent that came from experiences of your own parents, or from "cookie parents" who met your needs growing up, or from ideals in the culture.

To nurture yourself, you need to be attuned to your own needs and wants just as children need this from their parents. You might not need your diapers changed, but you certainly need support and comfort when you know you're in emotional distress. You no longer need to learn ABCs, but you need to learn the ABCs of coping when stress overwhelms you. You need to learn to pat yourself on the back when you do well and give yourself appropriate guidance when you've gotten off-track. When you mess up, you need to be gentle and nonviolent in the way you talk to yourself. In short, you nourish yourself from your Nurturing Parent part.

Here is a list to let you know if you're on the right track. The Nurturing Parent:

1. **Is a safe part of you.**
2. **Gives reality checks to the Inner Child through self-talk.**
3. **Is responsible for handling mistakes without indulging in guilt, shame, or blame.**
4. **Loves the Inner Child unconditionally.**

5. Loves others without exposing the Inner Child to victimization.
6. Listens to the Inner Child.
7. Takes care of the Inner Child.
8. Cares for the Inner Child without giving the Inner Child away to others.
9. Teaches the Inner Child consequences without needing to punish.
10. Will not be cynical, sarcastic, or judgmental.
11. Has a gentle, wise voice.
12. Allows the Inner Child to cry, show happiness, be angry or afraid, etc.
13. Nourishes even when the Critical Parent is present.
14. Understands the difference between healthy self-esteem and being self-centered.
15. Encourages healthy pride in accomplishment.
16. Will not allow the Inner Child to be victimized.
17. Teaches the Inner Child skills for survival, not cynicism.
18. Cares for the Inner Child no matter what else is going on.
19. Understands the Inner Child has needs to be met.
20. Allows the Inner Child to have independent thoughts and feelings.
21. Will never leave the Inner Child.
22. Recognizes and connects with the Inner Child's spiritual/religious part.
23. Supports the Inner Child's innate playfulness and curiosity.

If you review this list and fall far short of being able to be a Nurturing Parent to either your real life son or daughter or your own Inner Child, seek help. Talk to a mental health professional or take a parenting class or join a parent's support group. Call a helpline if you become so stressed that you are afraid of "losing it" and doing harm. I want to leave you with a lovely poem (it applies to both real kids and Inner Child parts).

If I Had My Child To Raise Over Again

If I had my child to raise all over again,
I'd build self-esteem first, and the house later.

I'd finger-paint more, and point the finger less.
I would do less correcting and more connecting.
I'd take my eyes off my watch, and watch with my eyes.
I would care to know less and know to care more.
I'd take more hikes and fly more kites.
I'd stop playing serious, and seriously play.
I would run through more fields and gaze at more stars.
I'd do more hugging and less tugging.
I'd see the oak tree in the acorn more often.
I would be firm less often, and affirm much more.
I'd model less about the love of power,
And more about the power of love.
—Diane Loomans

16
The Inner Child

It sounds corny, but I've promised my inner child that never again will I ever abandon myself for anything or anyone else again.

—Wynonna Judd

Caring for your inner child has a powerful and surprisingly quick result: Do it and the child heals.

—Martha Beck

More than 100 years ago the Swiss psychoanalyst Carl Jung wrote about the "Divine Child," a precursor to the writings of Irish spiritual leader Emmet Fox ("Wonder Child"), trauma physician Charles Whitfield ("Child Within"), psychiatrist/author Eric Berne ("Child"), and self-help educator John Bradshaw ("Wounded Inner Child"). All wrote extensively about the childlike aspect of the human psyche as an independent entity, and all considered that everyone has this aspect within them. This means there is still a young child inside the grown-up you.

I am writing about a simpler version of the Inner Child. The Child may be younger, such as four or five years of age, who is hurt, frightened, lonely and filled with shame. This Child wants to be held, wants to be validated, wants to belong, wants to be heard, wants a voice and, above all, wants to be loved. When she doesn't get what she needs and deserves, the Child becomes an angry teenager who is disrespectful and rebellious. When the Child suffers neglect or abuse, physical or sexual, then there is trauma, and as an adult will likely suffer symptoms of depression, panic attacks, addictions of all kinds, trust issues, eating disorders, dissociation, and post-traumatic stress.

If there is a symptomatic Child within the grown-up you and you are unaware of when she is running the show, you are more likely to end up unable to regulate your mood, panicky, comfort eating, spacing out, and not managing your relationships skillfully.

Think of your overall personality as different parts of you on the same bus. You want the Adult to drive the bus, but if the Inner Child gets behind the wheel, you are more than likely to end up upside down and in the ditch. For this reason alone, it is crucial that you become more self-aware and know when your Child has taken over. Then you can summon a more mature and resourceful part to be in charge. Here are some cues and clues that you are operating from your Inner Child:

1. **You feel little, like you did as a youngster, e.g., stomach in knots, afraid, ashamed.**
2. **Your voice becomes higher and sounds unsure, as if it's not coming from the stronger grounded center of yourself.**
3. **You feel unsafe and insecure.**
4. **You feel inadequate, not enough, incompetent.**
5. **You feel so driven to belong or be accepted that you would "sell yourself down the river."**
6. **You obsess about what people think of you and seek approval even if it means going against your opinion, morals, or values (a setup for codependency).**
7. **You have problems controlling your impulses, e.g., have sex with relative strangers, eat unhealthy food in excess, drink too much, gamble with money you can't afford to lose, yell when you should be modulated, run up credit card debt.**
8. **You are unable to regulate your emotions and moods, e.g., anger becomes rage, sad becomes a prolonged crying jag, anxiety becomes panic.**
9. **You act socially inappropriate, e.g., you say or do something embarrassing, you behave in a way that is universally judged as out of line, you trample another's boundaries. You shoot yourself in the foot.**

10. You experience no access to the Wiser or more Adult part of yourself, leading to poor judgment and ineffective communication.
11. You cannot trust your thoughts, feelings, or perceptions and must rely on those of others.
12. You feel lonely, scared, weak, fragile, or overwhelmed.
13. You take on guilt and shame even when you've done nothing wrong.
14. You "shoot yourself in the foot" or act in a self-defeating way (often the Rebellious Teen part).
15. You act entitled, as if exempted from the rules of society.
16. You see things in a self-serving way, and conduct yourself at the expense of others (not to be confused with healthy self-care).
17. You seem unable to discern reality, e.g., fail to notice obvious "red flags" in a new relationship.
18. You tune out self-awareness of your thoughts, feelings, desires, perceptions, etc.
19. You are afraid to try new things for fear of failure or to avoid discomfort.
20. You lose your problem-solving skills under stress.
21. You are in a situation where you forget how to negotiate, share, or take turns.
22. You suddenly act with a naiveté not consistent with your years of experience.
23. You can't set boundaries or you violate another's boundaries or are simply unaware of boundaries.

Study this list carefully to know when you've landed on or switched into your Inner Child. Do allow your Inner Child to play, create, recreate, sing, dance, laugh, be curious, explore, take risks, seek adventure, come up with fun things to do, and find wonder in the world. Do not allow your Child part to run the show and make important life decisions around issues such as relationships, dreams and goals, entering or leaving school, solving problems, choosing a mate, buying a house, deciding about a career, parenting, new purchases, old bills, or going through life transitions such as retirement or moving to another state. *If you feel like you are in your Child, you probably are.*

The Inner Child Worksheet

Natalie is a single professional woman in her mid-forties. To look at her, you would see a confident, together person who appears to be happy with her life. However, she fits the "looking good/feeling bad" profile as a result of her early developmental history. Throughout her twenties, as a result of childhood incest, she acted-out sexually, usually under the influence of alcohol or marijuana. Recently, her mother came for a weeklong visit, and Natalie chose to bring up the wound that occurred when she first disclosed her father's incestuous behavior. At that time, her mother refused to believe her, and Natalie felt another betrayal. This time, her mother believed her but more or less blamed her, which caused Natalie to spiral into depression and into a wounded Inner Child part. She raged at her mother and demanded that she leave on the next flight out.

Unable to contain her feelings, Natalie headed straight for the liquor store. The result was a five-day binge on Jack Daniels that blew six years of sobriety and put her in the hospital for detox. While her rage and grief were understandable, she did not express herself skillfully or regulate herself from an Adult part of her personality. In effect, she allowed the hurt, betrayed and overwhelmed Inner Child to drive her to the liquor store when she should have been calling her therapist and other members of her support system. She was triggered and tried to numb out her feelings rather than cope in a mature way.

Here are some tips when you realize you've slipped (are triggered) into your Inner Child and need to quickly get back into your Adult:

1. **Visualize your Adult** (it helps to have a vision of the strong Adult, looking solid, good posture, breathing deeply, your hair style, clothing, standing or sitting, where the Adult is now).
2. **Visualize stepping out of the Inner Child and stepping into the Adult.**

3. **Or, visualize the Inner Child walking over to the Adult and climbing into her lap to be held and comforted.**

4. **Tuck the Child into a safe and secure place** (a familiar and safe bed, a beloved grandparent's lap, by a warm fire in a mountain cabin, with friends or animals that love you).

5. **Have a wise spiritual archetype such as the Wise Old Woman join the Child** if the Child is fearful, hurting, confused, or feeling alone.

6. **Have the Adult take charge and retrieve the Child** after whatever needs to be done to remove the Child from harm's way.

7. **Have an inner dialogue between the parts** (as long as it takes to calm, reassure, and validate the Child).

8. **If the Child is stuck in and acting-out an unhealthy role, bring this to awareness and give the Child permission to step out of the old role.**

9. **Allow time for the Child to collect information** about how skillful, protective, and wise the Adult is and how much safer it is to let the Adult be in charge.

10. **Be aware you are likely to forget how to get from Inner Child to Adult,** so review this list regularly and practice getting big.

17
Green Is Good:
Turning Jealousy Into A Positive

Jealousy, that dragon which slays love under the pretense of keeping it alive.
—Havelock Ellis

Don't waste your dissatisfaction, use it as fuel.

—Thom Rutledge

Do you worry whether you're sufficiently attractive or successful to hold on to your partner? Do you compare yourself to others of the same sex and fear you could lose your partner to a rival? Is your sense of worth so low you feel you could easily be replaced in your relationship? If you notice your significant other looking at persons of the opposite sex, do you get a sick, vulnerable feeling? If you answered "yes" to any of these questions, you're struggling with the experience of jealousy.

It should be obvious that jealousy comes from feeling unworthy of respect and undeserving of love. These aspects of low self-esteem lead to a "jealousy triangle," composed of the jealous person, a beloved partner, and a rival. Three people are involved, whereas in envy it's usually two. Jealousy typically involves the desire to hold on-to what you already possess, whereas envy implies wanting something you covet, but don't have. For example, a wife is jealous of her husband's attention to the next-door neighbor and becomes watchful or possessive for fear of losing him. She is envious of the woman's new Mercedes. Her jealousy and envy make her unhappy and angry and can easily bring about the demise of an otherwise good relationship.

Most jealous persons believe it's their disposition or nature and that, once afflicted, they are doomed to act out jealously for life. Not true. Although jealousy looks entirely negative and destructive, recall that there are no gratuitous emotions. All have a purpose in guiding our social interactions and allowing us to respond appropriately to our circumstances. Jealousy is no exception and, with awareness, can be used in a productive and adaptive way.

An example will show us how. Muriel has been with her boyfriend Matt for more than two years. The relationship goes well enough but Muriel feels threatened by Matt's friendliness with other women at the gym where they work out. She is jealous of the time and attention Matt gives to anyone other than her. Muriel's choice is to allow her jealousy to consume her and spoil the relationship, or to use the feeling as a cue to resolve her insecurities. Here are some steps for Muriel to turn her jealousy into a positive for emotional growth:

1. **Be aware of jealousy and treat it like a cue**. (Muriel recognizes her jealousy is an indication of low self-esteem stemming from unmet needs in her family-of-origin).

2. **Identify which wants and needs are not being met.** (Muriel wants more of Matt; but simultaneously realizes he is doing nothing wrong in being friendly. She owns her problem, telling Matt she is going to work on it).

3. **Set up a plan to deal with her underlying issues.** (Muriel decides to watch her self-talk with the goal of improving feelings of worth. Whenever she is self-critical, she asks, "What is the evidence for that?" She disputes negative self-statements on a consistent basis and affirms her worth. She finds a good book on improving self-esteem and commits to reading it. She sets a realistic time frame for improvement and agrees to enter counseling if she can't do it on her own).

Jealousy is a common affliction and can often be handled with self-awareness and the following worksheet, but in some people the feeling becomes so corrosive it can wreck their relationships and lives. It would be misleading for me to suggest you can heal a serious jealousy problem after reading this brief chapter. I do however believe you can identify your problem here and seek out the counseling help you will need to work on the deep-seated inferiority complex that underlies pathological jealousy. This complex, which leaves you feeling inadequate, insecure, and threatened, is not your fault. It is a leftover from unmet childhood needs that can be corrected in a safe and corrective relationship with a good therapist. If you had a toothache, you'd go to the dentist. Smart people get help and take responsibility.

Green Is Good: Turning Jealousy Into A Positive Worksheet

1. Observe What Your Bodily and Emotional Cues Are during the experience of jealousy:

   _____

   _____

   _____

2. Notice What Your Self-Talk is and Replace it With Positive Statements:

   _____

   _____

   _____

3. Take the Energy From the Jealousy and Direct it in a Positive Direction:

   a. Ask yourself what your unmet wants and needs are based on reality:

      _____

      _____

      _____

   b. Make a plan and a list of what you need to accomplish to get your wants and needs met:

      _____

      _____

      _____

c. **Include a time frame of when these things will be accomplished:**

_____

_____

_____

d. **List the steps that you need to work on to accomplish your goals:**

_____

_____

_____

18
How To Be Vulnerable And Protect Yourself

Women are tenacious, and all of them should be tenacious of respect; without esteem they cannot exist; esteem is the first demand that they make of love.
— Honore de Balzac

When we are susceptible to a physical or emotional injury or wound we are said to be vulnerable. The adjective derives from the Latin equivalent *vulnerä*, "to wound." Wounds can come from criticism, emotional attacks, or actual weapons. Vulnerability also refers to being open to manipulation or maneuvering at times when we get weak-minded and give away our power.

Vulnerability is often considered a negative, but without it we cannot connect and love. Some people believe it's not possible to be vulnerable and protect yourself at the same time, but this is incorrect as long as you are in your Adult. If you have your Adult on duty you can be open, allow yourself to be seen (and thus vulnerable), and still mobilize your defenses if you sense immanent injury or have already suffered a wound.

So, in a healthy relationship you can be vulnerable and protected by staying Adult. In fact, it's hard to develop any kind of intimacy without being vulnerable. Making ourselves vulnerable, we must sometimes ask for help, admit feeling overwhelmed, take responsibility for a mistake, take our clothes off in front of a lover, express a desire for sexual contact, or call the doctor's office and request a lab report that could be scary. It's easy to see that we will face vulnerability when we expose ourselves to another because it means we risk disapproval, disappointment, frustration, criticism, embarrassment, humiliation, and a host of other painful feelings. It takes positive self-esteem as well as courage to make yourself vulnerable with so much on the line, otherwise the risk of exposure becomes too high.

Obviously, it's important in vulnerable situations to have boundaries and safety. If we are to show feelings, nudity, history, or private matters, we want to be with people who will not shame us, criticize us, or use the information against us. This is why it's so important to fix our pickers and make sure we connect with friends and lovers who are respectful and safe. If you are an emotionally sensitive woman or prone to shame, it's even more important to ensure safety before risking vulnerability. Don't throw your pearls before swine.

Amanda was a professional woman in her thirties, but naïve in terms of trusting people who didn't deserve it. Having gone to lunch with a new friend at work, an older woman who presented herself as together and trustworthy, Amanda shared that she had recently broken up with a long-term boyfriend for giving her a sexually transmitted disease (STD). In her own words, Amanda wanted to confide in someone and get some support. She made herself vulnerable because she wanted to be seen and connect to ease her emotional suffering. Her new friend appeared uncritical and sympathetic, but on returning to the office she proceeded to tell the story to another co-worker. Soon, everyone at her new place of employment knew the embarrassing truth, and Amanda felt utterly humiliated. Amanda "never dreamed she would blab something like that," but she had no reason not to trust the woman who injured her.

My work with Amanda was largely educational. We focused on a checklist of what needs to be present in order to protect oneself in vulnerable situations. Here is that list:

_____ **1. Find safe people.** Collect information over a reasonable period of time to ensure the person would not hurt you.

_____ **2. Find others who are genuine and authentic**; avoid the phonies.

_____ **3. Connect with people who are warm, nurturing, and compassionate.**

_____ 4. **Get close to those who also have the ability to be vulnerable and "seen."**

_____ 5. **Be honest with yourself when it comes to screening people**, friends, lovers, and potential partners.

_____ 6. **Take small steps to reveal personal information and see how others respond.** They must be discreet and respectful with any information you've shared.

_____ 7. **Open up to those who keep promises and who do not share information** with others unless given permission.

_____ 8. **Share with people who are non-judgmental or not critical of others or you.**

_____ 9. **Seek out persons who can be open to growth and to new, or different ideas.**

_____ 10. **Reveal yourself to people who are able to deal with different opinions.**

_____ 11. **Pay attention to how others talk about the people they know.** Are they telling secrets or sharing information that they shouldn't? Are they overly critical of others?

_____ 12. **Don't share information with others when you're under the influence** or when you know your judgment is poor.

_____ 13. **Be careful about sharing intimate information** during sex when you don't know the other person well.

_____ 14. **Take time and show patience** as you get to know anyone you want to be close with.

_____ 15. **Set limits and boundaries.** If you do not know your own, how can you set them with others? If others do not respond well to your established boundaries then they are not safe.

Do not let your Inner Child judge whether someone is safe just because you are lonely. Be sure and tell the other what to do or not do with the information you have shared, if appropriate. If there is a negative response to what you have shared, tell the other that their response hurt, not to do it again, and review if it is a good thing to share with that person again.

Amanda learned to take her time to more accurately discern if someone was safe. She would start with less revealing self-disclosures and see how the person responded. If she was criticized or judged, or the person violated her trust, she would pull back. If the person proved safe, she would try sharing something slightly more sensitive. She kept herself in check with self-talk like, "Don't share this yet. It's not time." Or, "I don't know this person well enough. Hold off. I can always tell them later if they prove to be safe." Only when the people in her life passed "trust tests" based on the list would Amanda open up to them. This saved her a lot of suffering going forward, as she had learned how to be vulnerable and protected at the same time. You can do it, too!

19
Predictability And Expectation:
An Emotional Protection

It makes sense to find a way to transform anything that has hurt us into a new experience that helps us.

—Gregg Braden

In keeping with author Gregg Braden's wise suggestion, I've found a way of transforming hurtful experiences into healing ones. My clients have dubbed this technique "P&E." The "P" stands for predictability, a person's observable pattern of behavior over a period of time. "E" stands for expectation, defined as how you expect a person to act or react based on past experience with them.

If you *expect* something outside the person's usual pattern of behavior, you will likely be disappointed, hurt, and/or angry. If your boss is typically disrespectful and you expect him to always treat you with respect, you're setting yourself up to be hurt. If you *expect* him to misbehave, you will be less likely to suffer. Example: Emily agrees to attend the Christmas party at the home of her parents. Her mother, a practicing alcoholic with a penchant for criticism, has spoiled many a family get-together after too many drinks. Indeed, she goes after Emily for bringing too small a casserole, but Emily expected it, so she's emotionally prepared and doesn't take it personally. She tells herself, "So Mom criticizes me at the family get-together. Big deal, that's what she does. It's about her, not me!" Or, "Birds fly, fish swim…Mom criticizes!"

Like Emily, when you *expect* something within the realm of the person's predictable behavior, you will be less likely to get hurt. That's living in reality, and it gives you time to plan an appropriate strategy about what to say, do, or expect. Consider Jack, whose father shows predictable behavior that includes obsessing, telling repetitious stories, and giving tedious lectures that question Jack's business decisions. This is his father's pattern and Jack expects it so he no longer gets angry and defensive when he does his thing. Instead, using P&E, Jack's plan is to keep his visits short and direct his father into other, safer subject areas, such as professional sports.

You can take it a step further by making a mental checklist and starting a game of predicting how many times a person will carry out their predictable behavior. For example, how many times will schoolteacher Aunt Ida correct your grammar? Or how often will a self-aggrandizing friend refer to how much more successful he is than you? Remember, humor is one of our most powerful coping strategies.

If a person does something positive that is outside their pattern of behavior, be pleasantly surprised and enjoy it, but don't change your expectations until an observable pattern change has occurred over many visits. People are capable of changing, but watch what they actually do, rather than simply trusting the words, "I've changed."

If you forget to use "P&E" and end up getting hurt in a situation where it could have been predicted and expected, remind yourself to do it next time. As you plan accordingly, it will reduce your pain and put the situation back under your conscious control. Your "self-talk" can be: "So what else is new?" or "Oops, I slipped, I guess I wasn't operating in reality." Nowadays, increasingly people are careless with their words and manners, especially with text messaging and social networking. I'm confident you will get lots of P&E practice. You will be amazed at what a difference it makes!

Predictability And Expectation: An Emotional Protection Worksheet

1. Situation:

_____

_____

_____

2. What do you expect?

_____

_____

_____

3. Are your expectations based on reality?_____

4. If not, what can you expect based on reality?

_____

_____

_____

5. What are your feelings about this (sad, hurt, angry...)?

_____

_____

_____

6. Realistic self-talk (It is what it is, so what can I do)?

_____

_____

_____

7. **Make a plan/problem solve:**

    a. **Pick a place to meet.** _____

    b. **Pick a time/amount of time (keep it short).**_____
       _____
       _____
       _____

    c. **What will I say?**_____
       _____
       _____
       _____

    d. **What will I do (Change the subject, leave, or disengage)?** _____
       _____
       _____
       _____

    e. **If I slip with my expectations, what can I do now?**

        • **Self-talk (should I be surprised? this is reality).**
           _____
           _____
           _____

        • **What can I do differently the next time?**
           _____
           _____
           _____

- **Humor/self-talk (Should I be surprised that this happened knowing he did this behavior ten times before? Oh, of course, what else is new? I wonder how many times he is going to do it the next time I see him?).**

_____

_____

_____

If you are not operating in reality, how can you plan or protect yourself? If you set yourself up with unrealistic expectations, who is to blame when others disappoint you? P&E will protect you!

20
Caring Is Not The Same As Carrying

Too often we underestimate the power of a touch, a smile, a kind word, a listening ear, an honest compliment, or the smallest act of caring, all of which have the potential to turn a life around.

— Leo Buscaglia

Caring for but never trying to own may be a further way to define friendship.

—William Glasser

To care for another is to hold that person in your heart, to feel and express positive regard as you invest emotionally in his or her life. Such caring is demonstrated in many ways, such as listening to the day's events, giving a supportive hug when things go badly, offering a prayer on behalf of the person, or just being present and helping out with whatever is needed - whether it's help with dishes, a ride to the doctor's office, a kind word, or a meal during a time of stress.

Carrying is defined as worrying on behalf of others and taking that person's pain inside of you. The carrier bears the other's burden and assumes responsibility for the other's issue, which incidentally, does the other no favor. This often occurs without awareness and results in the carrier feeling emotionally drained. Carriers then lack the internal emotional space to process their own life issues. Problems and unfinished business mount.

Example One: A *caring* mother has a chronically ill young daughter. She demonstrates caring by expressing her love, fixing chicken soup, massaging her back, reading her a story, and regularly checking in on her. All the while, the mother maintains balance in her life by eating and sleeping well, taking time to exercise, reading a good book in a favorite chair, and maintaining other relationships that sustain her.

Some mothers, however well-intentioned, would unwittingly *carry* a chronically ill child. These moms lose any semblance of balance their lives once had and suffer untoward consequences. They neglect their own self-care, isolate from potential sources of support, and often accumulate a laundry list of resentments that eventually turns into bitterness. Constant worry and preoccupation exhausts them and may result in physical illness or depression.

Example Two: A *caring* minister has a parishioner with an emergency. He has built time into his schedule for such contingencies. He listens attentively to the parishioner, shows his caring attitude by being fully present, responds actively and constructively, then the two pray together. The caring minister balances his personal needs, family life, and the demands of his congregation. His personal care includes setting aside time for contemplation as well as time with a friend or mentor to share the difficulties of his ministry. He eats well, takes a vitamin supplement, and enjoys his hobbies of cross-country skiing and golf.

A *carrying* minister stays up half the night, ruminating over the parishioner's problem. He can't eat breakfast because of a nervous stomach and resentfully struggles with the preparation of Sunday morning's sermon. Because he has little or no control over personal boundaries, his time is not his own. By not defining a self through limit setting, he has "lost himself." He allows parishioners to invade his personal and private space on an almost continual basis. Tired to the bone and brimming with resentments that cause him guilt, he sometimes questions his calling.

"Generational" modeling from family and friends teaches us that unless we *carry* other people's pain, we don't really *care*. This is simply not so. Care for those you love, but allow them to carry their own problems. That's best for both of you.

Correction

The burdens of the world
on my back
lighten the world
not a wit while
removing them greatly
decreases my specific
gravity.
> —A.R. Ammons

You can carry the message, but not the alcoholic.
> —Anonymous

21
Innies And Outies

Every good relationship, especially marriage, is based on respect. If it's not based on respect, nothing that appears to be good will last very long.

—Amy Grant

I want to be very close to someone I respect and admire and have somebody who feels the same way about me.

—Richard Bach

When it comes to respecting your boundaries and limits, there are four kinds of people. They are separated by their understanding that boundaries are to be respected, as well as their ability to take responsibility for the impact of their behavior. It takes a great deal of skill to know where I end and you begin. These descriptions will help you to decide who you want in your life (the Innies) and who you want to get out of your life (the Outies).

1. **Skillful and accountable.** Such persons will rarely violate your boundaries. If they do so it is by accident, and they will always own up to it. Then they make a mature apology and promise to be more respectful in the future and do so.

2. **Unskillful but accountable.** This person will violate your boundaries, but when confronted will own up to the transgression, make amends and strive to be more respectful. This person is not likely to violate your boundary again.

3. **Unskillful and not accountable.** When told they've violated your boundaries, this person may or may not own up to the transgression and is unlikely to make amends. This person is likely to violate your boundary again, not so much because they disrespect you, but because they just don't get it.

4. **Unskillful and disrespectful.** This person continues to violate your boundaries and limits no matter how many times you tell them. They refuse to take responsibility and are not likely to make amends. Instead, they deploy their defenses and may even make it your problem. Examples: "What's the big deal?," "You're too sensitive.," "Lighten up!," or "I was just joking." We have all come across people who push our buttons and "take runs" at our boundaries. Unless your self-esteem is rock solid, you don't want these people on your planet.

Awareness gives us a choice. We can choose to remain with or stay away from the kinds of people who inhabit these four categories. And, equally important, we can also choose which group we want to be in. This would be a good time for self examination, which of the four are you?

If we lose love and self respect for each other, this is how we finally die.
　　　　　　　　　　　　　　　　　　　　　　—Maya Angelou

22
Do's And Don'ts Of Internet Dating

Online dating can be fun and rewarding, but be cautious.
                                                    —Sharon O'Brien

For better or worse, millions of women and men and fully one-third of my clientele have tried Internet dating. And why not? After high school or college it can be hard to find men who share a common interest or who want what you want from life. If you proceed with caution and let go of the ideal of a "perfect match," online dating can be a good way to meet someone with a similar desire to connect. You can also make clear whether your intention is to find a friend to go to the movies with or to develop a meaningful, romantic relationship.

Whether you've already thrown your hat in the online ring or are just now contemplating such a move, you must educate yourself to increase your chances of having a safe and gratifying experience. Let's first acknowledge that to build a relationship we must make ourselves at least somewhat open and vulnerable and this will hold true whether we meet someone online or offline.

Mary, an attractive, well-educated professional woman in her early thirties, tried Internet dating on several occasions, but gave it up after two unfortunate experiences. The first one was more frustrating than harmful. She drove from western Washington to eastern Washington (four hours round trip) to meet a fellow with whom she'd been talking by telephone after an online introduction. Before agreeing to meet, she made certain Fred was at least six-foot tall, as Mary is five-foot-eleven, likes to wear heels and prefers men taller than she. Fred gave her his assurance he was six foot and even taller in his cowboy boots. As agreed, they met at the

Orange Julius in a downtown mall. To her utter disbelief, Fred was about five-eight. Mary was furious and his argument that height shouldn't matter did nothing to mollify her. To her credit, she told him that even if he was right, telling the truth did matter. He had no comeback to that one!

Mary's second bad experience involved a dangerous man. After several exciting dates with Benny, a handsome charmer with a Boston accent, she learned he had a criminal record and a number of pending court cases that ranged from aggravated assault to writing bad checks (red flag number #1). After doing some digging, Mary learned the company Benny claimed to own did not exist and that he also lied to her about his age (red flag number #2). When she confronted him with the truth, he verbally abused her (red flag number #3) and the relationship ended, but not before she suffered emotional harm. "How could he have lied to me?" she asked in our first session after the breakup. With good conscience development and a strong sense of fair play, Mary expected Benny to operate the same way she does. The problem is twofold: Benny has a type of personality disorder that leaves him with no moral compass, and Mary is too trusting by nature. She was so naïve she believed Benny would be honest with her. This experience shattered Mary's belief system and effectively ended online dating for her until we discussed a more enlightened approach.

Here is what I taught her. You can use the following ten tips to greatly improve the likelihood of a safe and rewarding Internet dating experience. The flipside? Ignore these guidelines at your peril!

1. **Use Fee for Service Internet Dating Sites.** The old adage "you get what you pay for" has to be right at least some of the time. The man of your dreams may be surfing the web looking for you, but take your time, use your brain, and don't trust him until he proves over time to be truthful and trustworthy. If he has to provide a credit card and other information to identify himself to a fee for service site, there's a greater chance he is who he says he is and a greater chance he is a person of character. The single, thirty-year-old personal trainer with 8 percent body fat and a heart of gold could be a forty-year-old, unemployed, alcoholic house painter with a wife and six kids. It happens.

2. **Meet in a Public Place.** Everyone agrees you make your first face-to-face meeting in a neutral public place (coffee shop, restaurant, park where there are people milling around) and depend on your own transportation (never ever let him pick you up at your home or accept a ride home until you get to know him better). Consider taking along a friend or setting up a way to have a friend check on you during the meeting or just after. Don't be afraid to ask a few nosy questions to verify he has told the truth in his online profile. Tell a trusted friend where you are and who you are with and why. *Do not confuse emailing back and forth or talking on the telephone prior to the first meeting as a way of really getting to know him.*

3. **Trust Your Gut.** Use your female intuition and gut instincts to screen any communication by email or phone, as well as face-to-face meetings. The only time your intuition doesn't work is the time you don't use it. If you get a "funny feeling" something is wrong, it probably is. If the hair on the back of your neck prickles, or you hear something that doesn't sound right, or discover information that doesn't match up, or sense energy that feels out of synch, or have a sense of unease without knowing why, it may be time to turn and run. If he seems to have a short fuse, or gives off a controlling vibe, or evades your questions, it's probably time to get rid of him. Don't put yourself in harm's way by ignoring red flags no matter how good he looks or sounds (refer to chapters *How to Recognize a Safe Person* and *Broken Pickers, Making Repairs*).

4. **Ask for A Recent Photo.** Ask for a photo but don't believe what it shows until you size him up in person. Those who argue it is shallow to want to see what he looks like are mistaken because you will waste your time and his if you are not attracted. If he tells you the photo is recent and then you meet and see he's gained fifty pounds and lost his hair, you will know he is not about the truth. Appearance can provide a feel for his personality and therefore is a way of knowing whether you want to proceed. If he takes off his shirt at the summer softball game and you notice his "Born to Kill"

tattoo, you have a red flag alert that must be attended to. At the least, there was a time in his life where he struggled with aggressive or violent impulses.

5. **Don't Give Personal Information Until You Are Ready.** Guard your personal information as one of your most valuable possessions. This includes your name and phone number. Wait until you are confident about the man to whom you're providing it. With today's search engines that do free background checks, giving out your full name and home phone number is about the same as announcing where you live, what your home is worth, where you work, and how much money you make. Scary, huh! If you decide to go from online anonymity to real email, use a free email account that isn't your usual one. Until you feel a real sense of safety from having met in person, block you phone number when you talk on the phone.

6. **Look for Red Flags.** It's easy to be fooled in the short run, so watch for red flags and deal-breakers. Here are a few common ones:
   - Pushes you to give up your online anonymity before you're ready.
   - Pressures you to meet before you're ready.
   - You feel a sense of unease or dread when he contacts you.
   - Doesn't want to talk on the phone with you.
   - Online profile doesn't match real life self-presentation.
   - Inappropriate touch during first meeting or too soon in relationship.
   - When he discusses failed relationships, he focuses entirely on "their" issues.
   - You've noticed or heard of his history of alcohol or drug problems.
   - Evasive answers to questions about job, marital status, children.
   - You see "potential" in him and think your love can "fix" him.
   - Your trusted friends don't like him and you make excuses.

- Doesn't have family or friends, or they are creepy and dysfunctional.

7. **Beware of Married Men.** Sadly, many married men cruise the Internet looking for sex or love. I've seen estimates that suggest that anywhere from 10 percent to 30 percent of men using online dating services are married. Remember, there are a lot of men with a Swiss cheese conscience, and until you've met him several times in person, he is a stranger. If he is evasive about his schedule or can only meet at odd hours, he may be hiding something important. If you're on the phone with him and he suddenly starts whispering or abruptly has to sign off, beware! Beware also of the man who admits to being married, but has been "miserable for years" and "in the process of divorcing." These guys are at the least emotionally unavailable and quite likely to be dangerous to your emotional and sexual well-being. If he lacks the ability to be faithful to his wife, he is not equipped to be in an intimate and satisfying relationship with you.

8. **Beware of Con Men.** A con man will earn your trust and then tell you a sob story about how he needs a little money for his sick child, sick mother, sick friend, or sick puppy. He's a scammer and a game player. If he even hints at wanting your bank or credit card numbers, break it off at once! If he just lost his job because the boss had it in for him or if he tells you an unscrupulous financial advisor just scammed him, look out. If your self-esteem is in the dumpster or you've been feeling desperately lonely, you are easy prey. Getting a little or a lot of attention can be very tempting, and you might convince yourself to stop collecting your information or ignore the red flags. A con man can sense your vulnerability, go into "chameleon" mode and provide whatever it is you think you need. Once he has ingratiated himself by making you feel better, he will cash in at your expense. By the way, con men know how to circumvent background checks, so don't automatically trust online services that advertise them.

9. **Avoid Cybersex.** Cybersex, also called net sex and other names, is a virtual sexual encounter, in which two people connect through a computer network to share a sexual experience. If you choose to participate in such activities you will find yourself role-playing and pretending to have sex with men or women who will almost certainly be masturbating. Exchanging sexually explicit messages in this way may seem exciting and even safe, but there is a risk of losing your anonymity and being either embarrassed or attacked. Net sex with someone you plan to meet is similarly a bad idea, as it sets up an expectation of what will happen when you meet in person. There are sexual predators that use the Internet as a dark alley to act-out their sexual fantasies in real life. Do not accommodate them no matter how emotionally or sexually needy you feel.

10. **Stay in Your Adult.** Throughout the process, stay in your Adult when you email, talk on the phone, meet, or date. The Adult part of your personality will collect information factually based on reality. If you put the Wounded Child part on duty, she will collect information based on need, and you will end up acting out issues such as abandonment, rejection, or abuse from your childhood. Your Child part has no business screening or communicating with strangers. She will ignore the red flags and set you up for chaos, danger, and misery. By all means ensure that it is your Adult part that decides if you are ready for sex. Before you do, ask him about the number of partners he's had and whether he always practiced safer sex (there's no such thing as "safe" sex in that there's always *some* risk). Ask frank, direct questions as to whether he's married or committed, separated, and whether he has any sexually transmitted diseases (and if they haven't had a recent test, make sure he gets one and shows it to you before you get naked together). If you can't be adult enough to talk about sex openly, you shouldn't be doing it.

Using the ten safety tips, Mary is having a better time finding and enjoying safe online dates. Knowing the dangers of Internet dating, she is always on the lookout for red flags and signs of trouble. Because she has slowed the process down and decided to be more realistic in her expectations, she has a better chance at becoming a "success story." She has come to realize that most of her dates won't pan out because that is the way the real world works. She has learned to accept that a man might not want a second date with her, just as she herself might choose to skip the second date if the chemistry is off. She uses her common sense and knows that more often than not she won't feel an instant connection. She sets the pace for the relationship, and she is the one who chooses him. She has learned to ask the difficult questions and is now making sexually responsible choices. By educating herself, she has significantly improved the quality and safety of her Internet dating experiences.

When I told Mary I was writing a chapter on online dating, she said, "Be sure to tell them not to push the river. It flows by itself!"

Do's And Don'ts Of Internet Dating Worksheet

1. Fee-for-service date site.

   _____

   _____

   _____

2. Meet in a public place or bring someone with you. Make a plan to connect with a friend during or right after._____

   _____

3. Trust your gut (what does your intuition tell you?).

   _____

   _____

   _____

4. Ask for a recent photo. _____

5. Don't give personal information until you are ready._____

6. Look for red flags.

   _____

   _____

   _____

7. Be aware of married men (ask questions).

   _____

   _____

   _____

8. **Be aware of con men (ask questions).**

   _____

   _____

   _____

9. **Avoid cybersex.** _____

10. **Stay in your Adult. Look for cues that you may be in your Child and shift back into your Adult. Good examples are feeling fear, experiencing high anxiety, having energized insistence, or scrambling for attention.**

    _____

    _____

    _____

23
Dating: Does Obsessing Help?

Be patient towards all that is unsolved in your heart... Try to love the questions themselves... Do not now seek the answers, which cannot be given because you would not be able to live them. And the point is, to live everything. Live the questions now. Perhaps you will then gradually, without noticing it, live along some distant day into the answers.

—Rainer Maria Rilke

Among men, sex sometimes results in intimacy; among women, intimacy sometimes results in sex.

—Barbara Cartland

A client of mine in her late twenties, Sarah, is struggling to understand how men think and relate. She has dated a succession of men who are slow in returning her messages and who seem less interested than she in setting a next date. Her assumption is that these men are either flaky or simply don't care.

Sarah's current dating interest is a handsome young man (handsome indeed, she showed me a photo on her phone) named Malik, who she met at a party for a mutual friend. Malik is from Iran and is in the United States working for a biotech company. From Sarah's description, he doesn't sound flaky at all. He sounds extraordinarily busy and devoted to his job. Sarah is obsessed with Malik, thinking about him all the time, wondering if he is attracted to her, asking herself and her friends if he is "the one," questioning whether she made a mistake by sleeping with him on their third date, replaying the lovemaking on their third date, worrying about how soon he will answer the text message she just sent him and what it means, wondering if there is another woman back home, wondering if he'd marry an American, wondering if his conservative Iranian parents would accept a foreign bride, and so on. Sarah is living proof that obsessing about dating makes things worse, not better.

I tried to settle Sarah down by reminding her it takes time to get to know another person and that Malik sounded very busy with his job. While empathizing that the pace was frustratingly slow for her, I suggested the pace might pick up after a few dates or if his work demands lightened. I told her to keep herself busy and have enough to do that she would obsess less with Malik. Time would reveal all and whether he was interested. If he proved to be a flake, she would learn soon enough. Meanwhile, go with the flow and exercise, write in her journal, call her friends, pursue her photography hobby, take a hot bath, do whatever she needed to do to regulate herself emotionally (as long as it was healthy!).

Most important, I asked Sarah to go inside herself and discover what was pushing all the obsessing. What did it say about her that she could only think of Malik and their future together after three dates? In doing this, we took the lid off her family-of-origin drama and discovered a childhood that left her feeling unwanted, abandoned, and insecure. I convinced Sarah that until she found some self-worth and self-love on her own that Malik, or any man for that matter, would pick up on her desperation and drop her for someone less needy. I showed her that worrying about someone and whether they care is tantamount to pounding sand down a hole. The other person may be swamped at work, may be poorly organized, may have poor follow through, may be secretly addicted to something, may prefer overweight women, may have had a recent death in the family, or maybe they just don't care.

To her credit, Sarah grasped this quickly. She realized that if she held on too tightly, most men would sense it and back away. If she pursued too strongly, most men would distance themselves. She made a real effort to stop obsessing about Malik and largely succeeded, just by monitoring her thoughts and doing a few breathing exercises designed to help her let go. When she found herself unable to stop the obsessing, she greeted it in a healthier way by reaching out to a friend or going to the gym to exercise.

She developed an attitude that Malik would either call her or not and that this was not under her control. She could only play her side of the net by contacting him and showing interest. When he was slow in responding she assumed he might be busy, might have another friend, might not be as interested, or any of many other possibilities.

Here are several tips if you find yourself obsessing about dating:

1. **Turn up your observer knob** (that part of you that observes yourself) and notice when you're obsessing.

2. **Practice supportive self-talk:** "This gets me nowhere." "This is not the way to start a healthy relationship." "I have a life and need to focus on positives, see friends, and do meaningful activities. I had these before I met him."

3. **Call a friend, but don't use the time by obsessing.** You may push them away.

4. **Turn, shift, and focus on something else.** Sometimes it helps to literally turn your body in another direction or sit in a different place to change perspectives.

5. **Go deeper.** Ask yourself why you are obsessing. Really, what is the commentary about you that you are doing this to yourself?

6. **If you can't stop obsessing, seek professional help** with a counselor, life coach, or minister.

Postscript: Malik turned out to be a "nice guy," and they were officially a couple for nearly two years. They visited his family in Iran and, in fact, he did not have his mother's blessings to marry an American woman. He stayed, she came home. She is not obsessing about what might have been.

Dating: Does Obsessing Help?
Worksheet

1. Notice obsessing (thought process and behavior).

   _____
   _____
   _____

2. Self-talk (common phrases that are helpful to you).

   _____
   _____
   _____

3. Talk to a friend about something other than obsessing.

   _____
   _____
   _____

4. Focus on something else (other thoughts or activities).

   _____
   _____
   _____

5. Go deep, and ask yourself what is driving your obsessing.

   _____
   _____
   _____

6. Get help (seek advice from counselor, minister, wise friend).

_____

_____

_____

Hope is a good thing as long as it is based in reality.
—Unknown

24
Sex Isn't Necessarily Intimacy

Sex is a poor substitute for intimacy.

—Dr. Mark Chironna

Intimacy develops more slowly, and commitment more gradually still.
—*Robert Sternberg.*

Sex and intimacy are not one in the same. To be intimate with another is to be open, close, and vulnerable, characteristics that may or may not include a sexual relationship. We engage in intimate friendships when we share our innermost feelings and deepest secrets without worry about being judged or criticized. For women this kind of intimacy is often shared with other women, and there is no sexual attraction whatsoever. So, sexuality is not necessary to define a relationship as intimate.

It's easier to develop a sexual relationship than an intimate one. For example, most women could at any time find a man to have sex with, especially in today's online environment and immediate access to sexual partners. Some women, especially those who confuse sex and intimacy, have tried using sex to connect and to meet emotional needs. Usually these needs are for attention and love but, time and time again, they come up empty. It takes time and effort as well as an intention to be close in order to cultivate a relationship that is truly intimate. To attain a relationship that is both intimate and sexual is even more difficult, but this is the definition of consummate love - a relationship that includes all the ingredients of friendship, trust, and sexual connection. Consummate love is what most of us covet and is well worth the effort. But it's not for the faint of heart (note our 55 percent divorce rate or the many unhappily married couples).

Sex can be fun and exciting but, I urge you not to use it as a substitute for close friendship, effective communication, and true intimacy. In my opinion, this is what happens with women who seek "friends with benefits" and often settle for sex without intimacy. This typically means that both parties have agreed to be sexual, but without any commitment or accountability. There are some inherent dangers to this newly minted approach. First off, one of the parties, usually the woman, may develop a real emotional attachment to her "friend" and end up heartbroken or feeling used. Another problem can pop up when real life sets in, and the woman becomes pregnant or one partner gives the other a sexually transmitted disease. I'm not a prude, and I believe people should have ways of getting sexual needs met even if they are unmarried, but proceed with great caution if you are in a "friends with benefits" relationship.

So, ask yourself what it is you want. Is it just a casual sexual encounter, or emotional intimacy, or both? Don't fool yourself. Make a conscious decision to seek either sex or intimacy or both simultaneously, but know that both work better if they begin with getting to know one another over time, as opposed to reckless behavior and drug or alcohol-fueled impulsiveness.

Know too that men and women have a different take on the meaning of sex early on in a relationship, say first, second, or third dates. Women tend to think that if they are sharing their bodies that an intimate encounter has occurred and that it means something positive about the future of the relationship. Men are more likely to see it as sex and view it as something happening in the moment without even considering the future.

This doesn't mean that men just want sex and don't want intimacy, which is an untrue and destructive myth in our society. But it does mean that women should be careful not to project what an early sexual encounter means to them onto the men they had sex with. Otherwise, she may be thinking, "He really cares about me!" while his mindset is more "She's a lot of fun!" Needless to say, these different interpretations of the same event can lead to some serious problems and high drama.

Here is a list I've compiled to help you differentiate intimacy from sex. Unlike sex, intimacy includes:

1. Love.
2. Attending to and tuning in to the other.
3. Trust.
4. Patience.
5. Friendship.
6. Sharing of self.
7. Authenticity.
8. Integrity.
9. Ability to maintain self over time.
10. Being able to set healthy limits and boundaries.
11. The ability to say 'no' without feeling guilty.
12. The ability to forgive one another.
13. Vulnerability.
14. Knowledge of the other.
15. Respect.
16. Honoring.
17. Safety.
18. Heartfelt relationship.
19. Expressing affection.
20. Soulful connection.
21. Deep, ongoing communication during good times and bad.
22. The ability to problem-solve.
23. Able to express feelings about unresolved issues.
24. Follow through over time (calling or checking in on a regular basis).
25. Continuity/consistency (personality traits are consistent over time).
26. Confidence to stay present.
27. Caring about the other person and their needs.

Sex outside of marriage or a mutually committed partnership is a personal choice for the reader. That choice should be based on:

- Safety.
- Talking about sex and what is expected (sex acts, preferences, what it means after the sex act). If you cannot talk about sex then you

seriously may be unable to handle the emotional consequences of your participation.

- Birth control (what kind, be prepared).
- STD prevention (tested and see results).
- Danger regarding encountering someone who is needy, obsessive, or dangerous.
- Personal values (what sex means or represents).
- Religion and moral compass (what sex means in a given religious context).
- Upbringing (what does sex mean?).
- Cultural practices (what is the meaning of sex?).
- Level of risk-taking (unprotected, bondage, location, under the influence, number of people involved).

So, you can have sex without intimacy and intimacy without sex. They need not and do not always go together. Whereas sex is defined as physical erotic touching and sexual union between human beings, intimacy is more about closeness, mutual respect, reciprocal love, authenticity, and a heartfelt relationship. "Hooking up" for a "one-night stand" may be sexually satisfying and fun, but it is surely not an intimate encounter. It's a whole lot easier to accomplish, but far less meaningful in the long run. Because men seem to have an easier time separating sexual activity and emotional attachment, women put themselves in an especially vulnerable position when engaging in casual sex. I suppose the salient question is: "What do I really want?" Be honest and then be true to yourself!

Love makes your soul crawl out from its hiding place.

—*Zora Neale Huston*

Nobody dies from lack of sex. It's lack of love we die from.

—*Mae West*

25
What Kind Of Passion Do You Have?

It is with our passions as it is with fire and water—
They are good servants, but bad masters.

—Roger L'Estrange

The happiness of a man in this life does not consist in the absence but in the
mastery of his passions.

—Alfred Lord Tennyson

Passion is an intense feeling about a person or a thing. It can also refer to a fervent interest in a given subject, an idea or a cause. Passion can be healthy or unhealthy, depending on its effect on the person who is passionate and its effects in the real world. For example, a person may have a healthy and passionate interest in advancing the beliefs and mission of the pro-life movement, but if they resort to threatening or assaulting doctors who perform abortions, they have crossed a line into the unhealthy.

Let's examine some of the variables that determine whether any particular passion is healthy or unhealthy.

1. **Conscious versus unconscious.** Staying with the above example, consider a woman who aborted a fetus at age fifteen, and now denounces and demonizes any woman who chooses to have an abortion. She wears hateful pro-life T-shirts, has a polarizing pro-life bumper sticker on her car, attends all the rallies and writes letters to the editor of her local newspaper that are so venomous they are not published. The vehemence of this woman's "passion" and certainty about a situation that she does not have all the facts about likely means she is being motivated by unresolved and unconscious forces such as guilt and shame.

2. **Spontaneity versus impulsivity.** It's one thing to have a healthy passion for adventure and to spontaneously join friends on a hiking trip in the foothills of the Cascade Mountains. However, if that same passion spurs you climb Mt. Rainier (at 14,410 feet, the most massive and extensively glaciated volcanic peak in the contiguous United States) without sufficient experience, training and conditioning, you have taken on an activity that is both impulsive and dangerous.

3. **Living in the moment versus for the moment.** To embrace a passion and live in the moment is healthy. It implies being present-centered and connected to the here and now. Marianne is passionate about wanting an intimate relationship. She wants to find a boyfriend she can love and who will give her the love she longs for. If she is living in the moment she is open to meeting men and connecting emotionally from a place that is centered and in touch with what is happening in the moment. Living for the moment is different and can cause you to lose yourself in the other person. Here, Marianne loses her center and allows her Child part to take over. Because she is ruled by emotion, she is swept away by unhealthy passion and ends up sleeping with a man she may never see again.

4. **Acting responsibly versus acting-out.** This is only slightly different from Marianne's example, but always implies action. To act responsibly is to keep an eye on your passion and to make good choices for the long-term. Acting-out is the attempt to meet emotional needs and resolve emotional conflicts through some form of action, whether it is responsible or not. Marianne is lonely and sexually frustrated, so she picks up a guy at a bar, even if it hurts her to do so. Acting-out is a self-destructive way to pursue a passion of any kind.

Notice in the above examples that unhealthy passion is full of energy and often related to obsessive or addictive behavior. It could be a derivative of a manic state or hyperactivity due to attention deficit disorder. No one feels freed up after acting on unhealthy passion, and it can undermine your self-esteem. Losing control of unhealthy passions, especially when your Child part is running the show, can negatively affect your health, family, friends, and job. By contrast, healthy passion feels more centered, calmer, quieter, and promotes positive self-esteem. It is energizing, freeing, and satisfying in the long run.

Pay attention to your personal cues and be mindful of the variables that determine whether you are into healthy or unhealthy passion. Make sure your Adult is on duty whenever passion is driving you because the possibility of emotional injury is high.

Ask yourself how you will feel if you indulge a particular passion. How do you feel before, during, and after engaging in your passion. For example, let's say you are passionate about rescuing feral cats and are going to a site to trap and neuter several animals. Before: "I have a sense of excitement and purpose!" During: "It's hard work, but I feel good about what I'm doing." After: "This is a good use of my time. I'm reducing suffering and making a difference!" Clearly, there is no reason not to proceed. However, if because of your passion, you decided to take eight abandoned cats and six kittens into your home and you lack the time and resources to make it work, you are engaged in unhealthy passion. If you're honest with yourself, the before, during, and after questions will tell you this would be a mistake. If your passions hurt you or someone else, then they are not healthy passions. Use the worksheet below to ensure yourself of making good choices.

What Kind Of Passion Do You Have? Worksheet

1. How does this experience make you feel?

_____

_____

2. What part of you is running the show in each category? Name the situation and indicate whether it is the Adult or Child.

	Situation	Before	During	After
1.	_____	_____	_____	_____
2.	_____	_____	_____	_____
3.	_____	_____	_____	_____
4.	_____	_____	_____	_____
5.	_____	_____	_____	_____
6.	_____	_____	_____	_____
7.	_____	_____	_____	_____
8.	_____	_____	_____	_____
9.	_____	_____	_____	_____
10.	_____	_____	_____	_____
11.	_____	_____	_____	_____
12.	_____	_____	_____	_____
13.	_____	_____	_____	_____
14.	_____	_____	_____	_____
15.	_____	_____	_____	_____

26
Never Be A Victim Again

Don't use the hardships of your past as excuses to deny the possibilities of your future.

—Robin Sharma

This above all, to refuse to be a victim.

—Margaret Atwood

That night was an especially exciting one for fifteen-year-old Bridget. She'd only just met Brandon, but he'd offered to pick her up at the south entrance to the mall and take her to a party in North Seattle. At seventeen, he could drive, an incentive that gave Bridget a little thrill, in and of itself. She arrived early and waited at the curb outside the food court, by herself, thinking about Brandon.

For reasons she didn't quite understand, Bridget felt apprehensive about this boy. Maybe because he seemed a little too cool and full of himself when they met at the skateboard park. Maybe because he was on suspension from high school for getting caught with a pint of vodka in his backpack. But it was silly to think there was anything wrong with Brandon, everyone she knew experimented with alcohol and, besides, the girl who introduced her to him said he was okay. She told herself to stop worrying. Worrying was what her mother did, always talking about how dangerous it is to be a teenage girl nowadays.

By the time Brandon arrived, twenty minutes late, Bridget had begun to wonder if she should get back on the bus and head home. She was about to leave when a pickup truck with fancy chrome wheels sped up to the curb and stopped abruptly. The passenger door flew open. Inside, the boy she'd met once grinned invitingly. Bridget climbed in and off they went, Brandon apologizing for being late. He seemed sincere, yet there was something that sounded wrong in his voice, or perhaps that was just her imagination. They drove to a residential area in Seattle and got themselves a bit lost, though that seemed weird too, because Brandon drove as if he knew exactly where he was going. Bridget told herself her mind was playing tricks on her, this driving with a boy and going to a party being so new and exciting.

When Brandon finally found the place, an expensive home in a nice neighborhood, they exited his truck and began walking up a flight of steps to the front door. Brandon walked ahead of her and too fast, which annoyed her and he appeared to be looking from side to side to see if anyone was watching. Oh well, that makes sense, Bridget reasoned. Teen parties rarely have parental approval, and he probably wanted to make sure they were arriving under the radar.

A clean-cut looking boy about her age or a little older opened the door and invited them in. There were four boys and only one other girl. That made Bridget a little uncomfortable, but after introductions were made she felt better. Besides, Brandon was paying close attention to her so she allowed herself to relax. Then she relaxed even more with a glass of red wine. She told herself not to have more than two because she didn't want to get drunk, but this wine seemed really strong and before she knew it she felt woozy. Fortunately, Brandon led her down the stairs and into the basement where she could lie down for awhile. He seemed so kind and concerned. She let him lay next to her on the bed because he promised not to touch her even if she passed out. But he broke his promise.

Bridget came to me at age eighteen, two years after the rape. For those two years she'd used the drug Ecstasy on an almost daily basis in a failed attempt to erase the memory of what had happened. By staying high, she avoided the maelstrom of negative feelings associated with such a horrific experience. I asked if she'd told anyone else what had happened and was not surprised when she answered no. She blamed herself for Brandon's criminal behavior and directed her rage at him back on herself. Only when I told her she'd been slipped a "date rape" drug did she begin to forgive herself for ending up isolated with a sexual predator.

Sadly, in the years between the rape and therapy, Bridget continued to put herself in dangerous situations. Therapists refer to this as "trauma reenactment." As is the case with many victims of rape, she felt undeserving of safety and unworthy of love. Troubled and suffering low self-esteem, she continued to date "bad boys" and was date raped on two more occasions after drinking too much. Not surprisingly, Bridget's presenting problems were the anxiety that comes with post-traumatic stress disorder and guilt over her sexual behavior. Fear permeated every aspect of her life, yet she continued to engage in high-risk behavior. Unless she could take better care of herself, the therapy wasn't going to work because she kept being re-traumatized. That made the first order of business with Bridget to teach her to stay out of harm's way. We adopted the following strategies:

1. **Pick safe people and safe places.** You deserve safety in every circumstance. If there is any question about a person or place, don't allow yourself to be compromised. Bridget agreed to give up the party life and avoid frequenting places where young people met to do drugs. Over time, she developed a new group of friends.

2. **Red flag the obvious.** Red flag any and all behaviors that make you feel anxious or uncomfortable. Confront the source of your discomfort and state clearly how you expect to be treated. Bridget went on three dates with a young man who refused to disclose what he did for a living. She liked him, but let him know his secretiveness made her nervous. When he refused to open up, she ended the relationship.

3. **Learn to say "NO!"** It is your right to assert yourself forcefully in any situation you suspect might lead to harm. This is how you reclaim your power. Bridget was enjoying a conversation with a young man who lived in the same apartment complex. When he pressured her to go up to his unit so he could show off his Sony PlayStation, Bridget felt an uncomfortable sensation in her stomach and refused. She simply said "No," and when he acted offended, she left the pool area where they'd been conversing.

4. **Know your boundaries and express them clearly.** We are safe within our boundaries, so if you are unaware of yours, discover them. It may sound cliché, but people really do treat us the way we train them to. Even during treatment, Bridget had a difficult time setting limits. She met a young man who attended a college almost two hours away. They hit it off, so she was willing to drive up to see him. But whenever she asked him to reciprocate he always had an excuse. Unwisely, she gave in by always being the one to travel. Her resentment grew and the relationship ended badly.

5. **Consider your choices.** Look for and consider all the choices available to you, rather than assuming you don't have any. Ask yourself, "How can I best respond to this person?" "What are my options in this situation?" One choice Bridget had not considered was to take some time off from dating to clarify her values and decide what she really wanted from life. When she did, she found an inner strength she did not know existed: an ability to be good company to herself.

6. **Reframe the way you look at things.** The same picture can look better in a new frame. Accept the fact that life is often unfair, grieve your losses, and move on. Bridget dropped the image of herself as a victim and instead chose to see herself as a survivor, able to extend heartfelt compassion and wisdom to others.

7. **Pick a healthy support system and put them to use.** If a red flag goes up, get the opinion of a trusted friend, family member, professional, minister or twelve-step group. Able to develop a trusting relationship with me, Bridget openly discussed her most vulnerable feelings. On occasion and with my encouragement, she would telephone me in between sessions for help with an immediate problem. This represented a huge gain, as she had unsuccessfully "licked her own wounds" her entire life.

8. **Practice good decision-making skills.** Without good decision-making skills, you may put yourself in compromising situations. With Bridget we used a stop-and-pause strategy before she made any decision that involved relating to the young men she attracted. During the pause she would consider her thoughts, feelings, and intuitions before proceeding.

9. **Collect information based on reality.** Get your facts straight. If you have to make decisions or take a risk, make sure your resources are factual. One of Bridget's most important lessons was to acknowledge that "some men can be trusted." This required her to make decisions based on fact rather than overgeneralization.

10. **Use your back end/front end skills.** If you can't say or do what you want on the spot, think it over and decide if you want to come back and say or do something later. Such back end work empowers you and increases your choices. As I told Bridget, "It's easier to answer the quiz show questions when you're at home." So don't be afraid to say, "I need some time to mull that over. I'll get back to you tomorrow."

11. **Give up your perfectionism**. Sometimes, we're so busy making sure others don't victimize us, we forget we can victimize ourselves. Learn to give it your best shot, then walk away or let go. For awhile Bridget did a one-eighty and sought the "perfect" boyfriend. He had to be trustworthy, respectful, supportive, ambitious, funny, cute, and a good dancer. Eventually she realized there are no perfect men (note: or women) and became willing to accept a young man who had most of the qualities she sought.

As children, many of us become victims because we are naïve and have no power. We are easy prey to the abusers and predators of the world. As adults, it is imperative we cease to see ourselves as victims, even if, like Bridget, we were tricked and exploited in the worst possible ways. When you define yourself as a victim, you forfeit your power and strength, leaving you vulnerable to the possibility of reenacting trauma scenes from childhood. This will almost certainly guarantee more traumatic experiences and more suffering.

In adopting the aforementioned strategies, the courageous Bridget redefined herself as a survivor, a young woman to be reckoned with. In time, she moved beyond the image of herself as a survivor to that of a fully functioning person who lives in the present and sees the world as rife with opportunity. She experiences herself as a part of that world, rather than as a "survivor," who is somehow separated from others. Bridget trusts herself and believes in her ability to recognize potential danger and take protective measures. She is currently dating a college classmate who treats her with consideration and respect. He can be clingy and demanding at times, but she does well in expressing her feelings and setting limits with him. They enjoy one another's company and have a lot of fun together. She continues to struggle, but she does so successfully in the sense that she no longer makes herself a victim.

Part Two
COMMUNICATION TOOLS

To disagree one doesn't have to be disagreeable.
—Barry Goldwater

Discussion is an exchange of knowledge; argument an exchange of ignorance.
—Robert Quillan

Silence is one of the hardest arguments to refute.
—Josh Billings

27
Communication And Problem Solving Skills

Communication breakdown, it's always the same,
I'm havin' a nervous breakdown, drivin' me insane!

—Led Zeppelin

Before you speak, let your words
pass through three gates.
At the first gate, ask yourself, 'Is it true?'
At the second ask, 'Is it necessary?'
At the third gate ask
'Is it kind?'

—Sufi saying

Effective communication is a door that swings both ways. A sender or speaker transmits the right message and a receiver or listener registers and understands it in a way that closely resembles its meaning and intention. When we communicate effectively, we send clear messages, we build instant rapport, and we are more likely to be "heard" and understood. It doesn't really matter whether we're talking with our best friend, loving spouse, difficult teenager, sociable neighbor, bossy boss, or a rude stranger, we must develop effective communication skills if we want a happy and successful life.

Communication breakdowns are all too common. Suppose Kathy starts a conversation with her husband that goes like this: "You better watch your drinking at the company Christmas party!" Taken aback and thrust into a state of stress, George responds, "If you think you're the boss of me, you're full of &#%*!" To state the obvious, there is a major communication breakdown between sender and receiver. Let's unpack what happened and how the communication could have been more effective.

First, Kathy would have been better off using a "soft startup," to borrow a term popularized by marital researcher Dr. John Gottman. This means, when you know the conversation is going to be emotionally charged, you initiate it in a gentle and kind-hearted way rather than coming out guns blazing and spewing criticism. Consider her "hard startup" ("you better watch") compared to a softer start that would begin with something positive. For instance, she could have said, "You've really made a good impression on your new bosses. I think we should be careful not to drink too much at the company Christmas party." This way she uses an "I" message rather than the more confrontational "you," and ends her communication with a clear and reasonable request.

A difficult conversation such as this one has a much better chance of going well with a soft startup. The way Kathy started got them off to a bad start, and it went downhill from there. George is less likely to take the message personally and also less likely to get defensive with the soft startup. He could now come back with, "Sounds like you're concerned about how much I've been drinking. Would you say more?" or something similar that would keep the lines of communication open.

Think of effective communication as a set of skills rather than a God-given ability or something that comes naturally with learning to speak. Many of us grew up with role models who unfortunately did not possess good communication skills and more or less programmed us with their bad habits. When we try to have a discussion that is emotionally charged we get activated, and so does the other person in the conversation. Things can spin out of control if messages are not duplicated and understood. The emotional brain can interfere with our ability to hear what was said. Sometimes we take it personally, sometimes we are overly sensitive, sometimes we get defensive, sometimes we insert our own agenda, sometimes we transfer feelings that belong elsewhere onto the sender, sometimes we are so busy rehearsing what we're going say we don't hear it all.

Life is all about having meaningful and satisfying relationships and this is only possible through clear communication. Below are some "skill-sets" and useful phrases to promote healthy and effective communication for individuals, couples, and families. These ideas can also be applied to the workplace and everyday conversation in public or private settings. Here are some principles of effective communication:

1. **Get clear on your thoughts and feelings before communicating.** If you're not ready to engage in a conversation you know will be emotionally loaded, ask for time to collect yourself or take a break. Be honest with yourself, there's no shame in needing preparation time to mobilize your skill-sets and rehearse. To increase the probability of a productive conversation:

   - Pick a non-stressful time with minimal distractions.
   - Pick a place that is safe and mutually agreeable.
   - Think through how you will use a "soft startup."
   - Keep it brief, don't belabor your points.
   - Don't throw in the "kitchen sink"(bringing up past issues).
   - Stick to the issue at hand and cue each other if you're wandering; "Let's stick to the issue," "Let's stay on target," "Let's get back to the issue," or "Let's work on the solution and work on these other points after."
   - Use "I" statements: " I feel this," "I believe," "I heard you say."
   - Use a calm voice. Monitor your tone and volume.
   - Be aware of your body language. Posture may be more threatening than words.
   - Avoid defensiveness, provoking and attacking the other. Do not use "you" statements.
   - If the discussion escalates, disengage. "This is not the best time to discuss this, this is not productive or constructive, let's set another time to talk." This is not avoiding the issue as long as a follow-up time is set.

- Time outs are useful to collect your thoughts, recover your "calm," and explore possibilities.
- End the conversation with a clear and reasonable request for what you want or need.

2. **Agree to Disagree.** No one has the absolute take on reality so be willing to accept that not everyone will agree with you. If you always try to pull the other over to your side, you will invite resistance and arguments. Try to show some curiosity for the other's point of view no matter how vehemently you disagree with it. Not every subject has to be negotiated and agreed upon, so embrace the differences and move on. "We can agree to disagree." "It's alright that we disagree, disagreement is okay, we can have our own point of view."

3. **Listen, Acknowledge, and Validate.** Give the other their opportunity to express themselves and try to see their point even if you disagree with it. Defensiveness and argumentativeness undermines effective communication and creates resentment. It's not necessary to understand the other's point of view; however, it is essential to honor and respect their opinion! "I heard you say . . ." "That must have been difficult," "How can I support you?" "That's a good point." *Don't forget to share air time.*

4. **Clarify.** Get clear about what "words" mean. Often couples agree on an issue, but argue about a difference of interpretation. "Is this what you mean?" "I don't understand." "Can you try saying it in a different way?" "Are we saying the same thing? "Help me to see it." "I'd like to get clear on this."

5. **Problem-Solve, Negotiate, and Compromise.** Even schoolchildren learn to take turns on the playground. This does not mean that you're "giving in," "giving yourself up," or losing. Try to arrive at a mutually respectful agreement in which all parties experience a "win-win" situation. People's combined years of experience

represent a pool of creative ideas from which to draw upon. "Let's work in the solution," rather than "my way or the highway." "Let's get creative…Let's throw some ideas on the table…What ideas do you have…Here's some ideas that I have…Let's take turns." Offer and counteroffer.

6. **If a fight or disagreement erupts, repeat the above process.** Take note, if you get stuck on one or more steps, practice those steps before continuing. If you find that you cannot continue, and these suggestions are not enough, consider counseling with someone who has expertise in working with communication skills.

The first one to get angry loses.

—Anonymous

The way to remove darkness from a room is simply *to turn on a light. In the same way, to rid yourself of any difficulty, concentrate on the* solution *rather than the problem.*

—Zen saying

A note on learning styles:

It's important to understand there is more than one way to learn. Not everyone receives, processes and ultimately acts on information in the same way. If you're going to communicate effectively and minimize conflict, you want to develop an appreciation for learning styles that are different than your own.

To do this, gather information about how a person would best receive and understand what is presented to them. If appropriate, ask them how they learn best, or try out new strategies of presenting ideas. A friend told me recently how she flunked a test to become a bus driver. She "just couldn't memorize" all the information they threw at her, some of which was mechanical and technical. I had her show me the material. Her method was to read and memorize, which wasn't working. I had her draw pictures instead, and then I read the information to her, thus using a different channel to get the information into her memory banks. She passed the test on her next try.

There are many different kinds of intelligence. School tends to tap into word smarts and math smarts, but not everyone is smart in these ways, and students may lose self-esteem and self-confidence. Instead, they may be logic smart, or music smart, or art smart, or people smart, or have other open channels for learning new information. Like the Zen saying reminds us, focus on the solution. Try presenting a picture, draw a diagram, or make a list. Write a song or limerick or put the information to music. Use tangible objects, move pieces on a chessboard, tell a story and physically experience what is being discussed. An example of that would be a couple negotiating building their dream home by looking at home magazines together or drawing out a design. Trial and error will help you get to know how you can relate to the person best. By doing so, your communication and negotiation will go more smoothly.

When my daughter was young and had a chronic illness, I would intuitively know by glancing at her whether or not she needed to go to the hospital. This vigilance was a day and night affair. It was critical for my daughter's survival to make accurate, timely and effective decisions. When I told my husband what to look for when "on watch," he *could not* read the symptoms by simply looking. This was not only a life-threatening situation, but it confounded and challenged my understanding of his lack of response. I decided I needed a better understanding of his learning style. I asked myself what would be the best mechanism for him to be able to screen her symptoms. Since he operates best by using lists, we made up a list of ten symptoms. From that point on, he became an expert at recognizing symptoms and making effective decisions about our daughter's treatment.

In the end, communication skills come in all forms and are directly linked to the success of negotiation and problem solving. How information is received is as individual as the fingerprint. Creative combinations of one, some, or all suggested methods may be necessary to communicate your ideas. Having an appreciation of different learning styles is well worth the effort.

Communication And Problem Solving Skills Worksheet

Where do you get stuck?

1. **Get clear on what you want to say:**

    _____

    _____

    _____

2. **Best time to talk:**_____

3. **Best place to talk:**_____

4. **Soft start-up:**_____

5. **Keep it brief:**_____

6. **Avoid throwing in the "kitchen sink:"**

    _____

    _____

    _____

7. **Stick to issue and use cues:**_____

8. **Use "I" statements:**_____

9. **Use calm voice:**_____

10. **Use non-threatening body language:**_____

11. **Don't be defensive or provoke it:**_____

12. **Use disengaging:**_____

13. **Timeouts:**_____

14. **End the conversation with a reasonable request:**_____

15. **"Let's set another time:"**_____

16. **Initiate the next meeting:** _____

17. **Agree to disagree:**_____

18. **Listen, acknowledge, validate:**_____

19. **Clarify:**_____

20. **Work to problem-solve, negotiate, and compromise:**

_____

_____

_____

21. **Awareness of learning styles:**

_____

_____

_____

If a fight or disagreement breaks out, repeat process or get professional help.

The test of a first-rate intelligence is the ability to hold two opposing ideas in mind at the same time and still retain the ability to function.

— F. Scott Fitzgerald

Sometimes, my greatest accomplishment is just keeping my mouth shut.

— Unknown

28
The Pearl-Handled Pistol: Moderation When Finding Your Inner Voice

Speak clearly, if you speak at all; carve every word before you let it fall.
—Oliver Wendell Holmes

Do not remove a fly from your friend's forehead with a hatchet.
—Chinese proverb

"I'm just horribly depressed!" exclaimed the middle-aged woman on my couch. "And I don't even know why!"

I could tell there was something sad about Melinda when she phoned me for an initial consultation. I could hear it in the tone of her voice more than in the content of her words.

"My husband, Larry, and I moved up here twelve years ago. He got on at Boeing so we moved from Louisiana, where all my family is. And I hate it here. I can't take the rain and all the gray days . . . it gets to me every winter. Larry says I need to learn to accept it, to look around and see how beautiful it is and to stop complaining so much."

"Do you think he understands how unhappy you are, how depressed you've been feeling?" I asked her.

Her body slumped and she broke eye contact. "I don't know. Maybe. He knows I started taking antidepressants years ago. But he likes the Northwest. And the money's good at Boeing."

"How long have you been unhappy here, Melinda?"

"Since the day we arrived. But I thought I could get used to it. I guess there's something wrong with me."

"What do you want?" I asked.

"What?" She looked as if I'd asked a shocking or inappropriate question.

"Yes, what do you want? What would make you less depressed and more happy?"

There was a rather long pause at this point. Finally, Melinda said, "I've never asked myself that."

"Maybe that's why you're here," I replied.

"It wouldn't make any difference," she said. "Larry would never move, anyway."

"Maybe not, but at least you'd have said how you felt. And, who knows, maybe it would make a difference. Especially if Larry knew how miserable you are."

Finding your inner voice is a real skill, and an art form when you cultivate authenticity. In our next two sessions, Melinda and I explored her true feelings and the depths of her depression. She began to accept the idea it was okay for her to want to move back home to Louisiana, even if it would displease her husband to think this way. She realized that she had allowed herself to be defined by Larry and what he wanted her to be, rather than who she really was. When Melinda shared how frightened it would be to displease him I asked her how old she felt.

"About ten," she answered, without hesitation.

Now I coached her up and got her to stay in her Adult part during any conversation with Larry, as the wounded and accommodating ten-year-old wouldn't stand a chance of getting what she wanted. By identifying her wants and needs and values and by remaining Adult, Melinda reconnected with her true self and, not surprisingly, began to feel better.

Now came the hard part. She'd become aware of her inner voice and what she truly wanted. But could she find the courage to communicate this to Larry, who was bound to be disappointed and angry? We talked about authenticity, about the importance of "showing up" in her marriage and being willing to be herself. After several more sessions of role-playing and rehearsal, she went home and opened up to Larry. Here is the gist of what she said:

"Larry, it scares me to bring this up, but I have to be honest with you. I am so desperately unhappy here that I want to move back to Louisiana. I've tried, but I just can't get used to the weather and to being so far from my family. And you told me you could get work in Baton Rouge. And yes, you'd take a pay cut, but the cost of living is way less there and you'd have a happy wife."

To say the least, Larry was not receptive, so Melinda continued with Plan B.

"Okay," she told him, "you have every right to want to stay here, but I have every right not to stay with you. Unless we make plans to move by the end of the year (this was September), I will move on my own. We will just have to separate."

"Are you threatening me?" he asked, incredulously.

"No, I'm making you a final offer. I've given it . . . I've given *you* twelve years here, and I can't do it anymore. I love you and I want you to come with me. You have to make a choice."

Note: Larry called her 'bluff' only to find it wasn't a bluff. Melinda, the resourceful and grownup woman, moved to Louisiana at year's end. Larry was at first stunned but, to his credit, accepted her influence and joined her three months later. Their relationship has changed and is much more equal now. Larry is not always happy with the changes. Melinda has never been happier.

Many women who find their inner voice are too frightened to be as expressive and authentic as Melinda. Others move into anger and go too far, either with their words or their actions. There is a place in between fear and anger, between passive and aggressive that is just right, a moderate place where you stay Adult and stay centered. When we are open and direct, but still centered and gracious, we arm ourselves with a tool I call "the pearl-handled pistol." This tool not only makes us happier and more satisfied, but also helps us with intimacy, boundary setting, problem solving and protection. It must be used carefully, as "going off" will certainly make things worse. In other words, it requires some practice in using it properly, graciously making yourself known by expressing your innermost feelings.

The pearl-handled pistol works for boundary setting as well as expressing wants and needs. A young woman recently told me that a male co-worker would touch her bottom at work and then blame her for bumping into him. She told him to stop, but he refused to honor her boundary. Now is the time to up the ante by saying something firmer (sort of like brandishing the pistol without firing it). She informed him that if it happened again she would first dial 911 and summon the police and then report the creep to management. It never happened again. She did it all with a calm voice, graciously. She looked him squarely in the eye, but didn't have to yell at him or be militant. She just owned her inner voice and let him know she meant business.

Here are some more ideas on how to find your voice and wield the pearl-handled pistol:

1. **Use your observer part** (the part that notices every aspect of your experience, but without judgment) to become aware of what's happening with you. Ask yourself if you are in your Adult?

2. **Assess the situation:**
   - What am I feeling?
   - What am I thinking?
   - What am I doing?
   - What are my wants and needs?
   - What are my values?
   - Are my boundaries being honored or violated?
   - Validate your experience ("I have the right to feel angry," "I'm entitled to want a commitment," or "I have a right to have my boundaries respected!").
   - What do I need to say to express myself authentically?
   - How do I best educate the other person?
   - Am I expressing myself to a safe person?
   - If not, am I in danger? If so, then consider whether expressing yourself is the wisest choice and mobilize all resources at hand.

It's important to notice that in order to advocate for yourself as effectively as this young woman you must first validate your experience. This means you corroborate what is happening to you and support the soundness and legitimacy of your feelings, thoughts, and reactions. In this case, it meant she said things to herself such as, "I have every reason to be offended by his actions," or "I have free and clear title to my body so no one gets to touch me unless I am okay with it; therefore, I'm entitled to be furious by this jerk's inappropriate behavior." Had she instead told herself, "Boys will be boys," or "It's not that big a deal," she would have invalidated her feelings and been unable to act assertively on her own behalf to stop the violations.

Sometimes when women first find their inner voice, they have problems assessing how firm and loud they should be. Please use this worksheet and chapter to assess what would be a fitting response to whatever situation comes up. It is authenticity that gives you the chance to be yourself and obtain what you need to feel happy and fulfilled.

The Pearl-Handled Pistol: Moderation When Finding Your Inner Voice Worksheet

1. **Situation that may require the pearl handled pistol:**

   _____

   _____

   _____

2. **Am I in my Adult?** (If not, my plan to summon most grown-up, resourceful part.)_____

3. **Assess the situation.**

   - What am I feeling, thinking, doing, wanting, needing, valuing?

     _____

     _____

     _____

   - Are my boundaries being honored or violated?_____

     _____

   - Self-talk to validate my experience._____

     _____

   - What do I need to say or do to express myself authentically? _____

     _____

- Best way to educate the other person:_____
  _____
  _____
  _____

- Am I expressing myself to a safe person? If not, then use all resources at hand to ensure safety.
  _____
  _____
  _____

4. **You can use "back end" skills to come back and tell the person** if you don't catch it at the "front end" (See the chapter *Front-End, Back-End Work*).
   _____
   _____
   _____

5. **Pick the time and place to use your voice.**
   _____
   _____
   _____

6. **"Do I need to get out the pistol and show it?"** (How firm and loud should this message be?)
   Gracious request_____
   Firm demand_____
   Firmer demand_____
   Ultimatum_____
   Loudness 1 2 3 4 5 6 7 8 9 10

29
The Fire-Breathing Dragon: Taming Abusive Anger

If you are patient in one moment of anger, you will escape a hundred days of sorrow.

—Chinese proverb

Let's not get rid of our anger, it has survival value. Anger calls us to our battle stations to meet an annoying intrusion or perceived threat to our safety, whether physical or psychological. It is therefore a positive emotion, informing us when we need to set a limit or prepare a defense. This is healthy anger, enhancing our communication and providing protection. Examples: your boyfriend calls you a "selfish bitch" and you tell him he has abused you and the relationship is over. Your neighbor repeatedly allows her terriers to trample your flower beds and poop on your lawn and you ask her to confine them or risk a report to animal control. Notice how healthy anger functions like an arrow, directing you to take appropriate actions on your own behalf.

Lydia, a college graduate in her early twenties, was referred for anger management. A Native American raised on the "Rez," Lydia often thinks about the land that was illegally taken from her people. Understandably, there is a part of her that feels enraged over the injustices done to her people. In our first session, she disclosed a history of fighting with white girls in high school. She was court ordered to see me after an incident at an outlet mall. There, Lydia got involved in a dispute over a parking place and bloodied the lip of a Caucasian woman. What started out as healthy anger had metastasized into rage, gotten Lydia in its grip and convinced her to act out. I asked her if she'd have struck this woman had she been Native American and Lydia answered "no." Not only had she gotten herself in trouble with the law, she had stereotyped an entire group of people, duplicating the type of wrong done by racists to her own people. In order to help Lydia, I had to convince her the problem was not that this white woman had taken a parking place that belonged to Lydia (the unconscious meaning here is painfully obvious), but the way she thought about this white woman taking the parking place she believed was rightfully hers. To her credit, Lydia got it and changed her way of thinking.

Cognitive psychologists tell us that thoughts precede emotions; for example, thoughts of danger generate fear and thoughts of trespass generate anger. According to this theory, the way we think about and interpret the past has much to do with the intensity of our emotion. When I first started doing psychotherapy, I encouraged my enraged clients to ventilate and they were more than glad to comply, pounding pillows and screaming epithets at those who victimized them. But my clients didn't often improve; in fact, they dwelled on their feelings of outrage and some became even angrier. Now I teach people to change their thinking and detach from intense and vengeful thoughts. I encourage them to consider their thoughts and how they make them feel and then decide if they really want to stay attached to them. And it works. By learning to watch your angry thoughts rather than judge them, analyze them or act them out, they dissipate and free you up. By learning to detach from angry thoughts and use their energy to take care of yourself, you make your world safer and more satisfying at the same time.

Here are some strategies to keep your anger on the healthy side of the ledger:

1. **Take a time out.** Sometimes our anger feels like it's too much to contain. We feel overwhelmed or enraged and anger spills over in ways we regret. When your anger is too intense to be used in a positive or productive way, you can take a time out and follow these suggestions:
   a. Breathe deep into your tummy and cool down.
   b. Decide to not strike while the iron is hot.

c. Take the one action that will best solve your problem.

d. Stay focused on what you can do, not on how helpless you feel.

e. Let it go (after acting or expressing your anger).

2. **Take care of yourself when stressed.** Attend to thought processes, bodily sensations and emotional cues that tell you you're overloaded. Be aware of stressful environmental factors such as job demands, too much to do, losses of any kind, deaths and major life transitions. Lydia came to realize she was especially prone to acting out anger when she allowed herself to become fatigued. Develop a routine that works for you to lower stress – savor a cup of herbal tea, enjoy a bubble bath, burn candles, exercise, meditate, pray, read for pleasure, inhabit a quiet space, talk to friends, listen to soothing music, breathe deep down into your tummy, watch favorite reruns and have a good laugh. Experiment and learn the most effective way for you to lower stress, then write it down and follow it.

3. **Attend to physical or medical issues.** If you suffer from a chemical imbalance that affects your moods (a "no-fault" brain disorder), get medical help with antidepressants, herbal remedies and talk therapy. If you have learned to self-medicate with alcohol, drugs or food, acknowledge the problem and make a plan to deal with it. Lydia acknowledged being most irritable when pre-menstrual and found help by taking Prozac. Smart people get help!

4. **Change your self-talk.**
   a. "I don't have to take it personally."
   b. "It's not what he did that makes me mad, it's my reaction to it."
   c. "This is not about me."
   d. "This is what I'd expect from a disrespectful teenager."
   e. "I'm taking a time out before discussing this."
   f. "I choose to turn this over to my Higher Power."
   g. "This is not a good time to deal with this."
   h. "I can let it go."

      i. "It's not worth it."

      j. "I need to stay adult."

      k. "Don't go there now."

      l. "I won't go into my lower self just because he did."

5. **Express yourself to others.**

    a. "This isn't a good time for me."

    b. "Let's take a time out and set up another time."

    c. "Let's come back to this after we've cooled down."

    d. "I'm tired and it has been a bad day. Can we set another time to talk?

    e. "I love you."

    f. "I have feelings too, let's not hurt each other."

    g. "Let's stick to the issue. We can talk about other issues later."

    h. "Let's not say things we'll be sorry for."

    i. "I disagree, but I'm interested in your opinion."

    j. "Let's agree to disagree about this."

    k. "In the future, if I say 'stop,' I expect you to take that as a cue that I'm not willing to continue the conversation until a later date and time."

With awareness and understanding of ourselves, we have the choice of giving in to or standing up to anger. When we give in, our anger can become a fire-breathing dragon that damages our relationships and our lives. We forget who we really are – women who are peaceful, loving, and gracious. By following the above strategies Lydia learned to disengage and use anger constructively. Like Lydia, you can opt to leave an angry discussion, write an angry letter with no intention of mailing it or take a brisk walk. These are far better solutions than acting out. The way to tame anger is to avoid striking while the iron is hot and then to reengage after collecting yourself. Lydia now channels her healthy anger working for a nonprofit organization that teaches Native American children to protect themselves from victimization.

30
Protect Yourself And Let Go Of Your Anger

Not the fastest horse can catch a word spoken in anger.

—Chinese proverb

The Zen of Horse Sense

Off the Northwest coast of the United States is an archipelago called the San Juan Islands. From one of the mountaintops you can see Canada, the United States mainland and all the little islands in the San Juan chain. Lush vegetation and abundant wildlife characterize these islands.

People come from all over the world to enjoy this magnificent view so when attendance dropped dramatically, the park ranger went out to discover what was wrong. Standing at the park entrance was a proud buckskin mustang biting and kicking anyone who dared come near.

The park ranger approached the wild horse and, with great authority in his voice, said, "If you don't stop biting and kicking the visitors, I'll have you relocated to a zoo." An intelligent animal, the horse realized the ranger meant business and vowed not to display any aggressive behavior.

The tourists came back in droves, but when the ranger went to check on the horse he found him beaten down and depressed. His once beautiful black mane and tail had lost their luster and he no longer carried himself with dignity. On questioning, the horse explained that children had pulled his tail and people had thrown rocks and mud balls at him.

"Why didn't you defend yourself?" the ranger asked.

Dejectedly, the mustang answered, "Because you told me you'd ship me to a zoo if I bit or kicked the tourists."

"Yes," the ranger acknowledged. "But that doesn't mean that you can't flick your tail, flatten your ears, stomp your foot or snort through your nose. This will let them know they can't abuse you."

This story teaches us to use anger to protect ourselves without harming others. But some people struggle to let go of anger and can't because they fear they will be vulnerable to being hurt again. When my clients voice this concern, I tell them: "If you have the right skills for protection, you can let go of your anger."

Here are the skills:

1. **Get your facts straight.** Collect your information about people in reality and take your time doing it. Ask yourself, "Is this person safe?" That way you won't go off half-cocked.

2. **Speak up about your needs.** Let people know what your boundaries are and what you want from them. Write out or practice how you want to deliver the information.

3. **Walk away from hurtful situations.** Disengage from escalating circumstances and wait for things to cool down.

4. **God never hurt you.** That's not how God operates. You do not have to protect yourself from Him. If you believe God hurt you, talk to God, reexamine your beliefs, grieve your situation and move on.

5. **Have realistic expectations of what another person can and will do.** Don't set yourself up for hurt and anger by expecting an abusive person to be kind and considerate.

6. **Remember we live in a gray world.** Black and white thinking is a dangerous game. Evaluate others as whole persons and don't just write them off for one aspect of their personality, but at the same time protect yourself.

7. **Set limits to ensure your safety.** You are a different person, stronger and wiser because you learn from your mistakes and operate in reality.

8. **Use your Adult part rather than your Inner Child to handle matters of vulnerability.** Your "child" may be incapable of self-expression in situations where your "adult" knows just what to say and how to say it.

Protect Yourself And Let Go Of Your Anger Worksheet

Use the following worksheet to devise a more effective strategy for self-protection.

1. **Get your facts straight.** _____

_____

_____

_____

_____

2. **Speak up about your needs.** _____

_____

_____

_____

_____

3. **Walk away from hurtful situations.** _____

_____

_____

_____

_____

4. **God never hurt you, let go.** _____

_____

_____

_____

_____

5. Have realistic expectations of other people. _____

_____

_____

_____

_____

6. Evaluate the person as a whole. _____

_____

_____

_____

_____

7. What are your limits? _____

_____

_____

_____

_____

8. How can you be mature about this? What would your strategy be to engage with the other person? _____

_____

_____

_____

_____

31
Beneath The Surface Of Anger

Here in the world, anger is never pacified by anger. It is pacified by love. This is the eternal truth.

—Buddha

Between the inevitable stresses of life in general, and annoying people in particular, we are often drawn into our lower selves. The lower self, the most reactive part of us, is like a powder keg waiting to explode and every day we encounter sparks. An inattentive and dangerous driver is a spark, a family member who speaks unkind words is a spark, a setback at work is a spark, a child who behaves badly in public is a spark, a jealous and possessive life partner is a spark, harsh criticism or judgment from almost anyone is a spark, the memory of an unresolved traumatic experience is a spark. I could go on and on, there are literally hundreds of situations that can spark us to anger.

Yet often when we display anger, it is not our primary feeling. If I kick you hard on the shin you get angry, but first it hurts. Hurt is the primary emotion and anger is secondary. It's easier and less vulnerable to say "I'm angry" than "I'm hurt." The hurt remains hidden and often unexpressed. There is a cost if the hurt stays under the surface. The unacknowledged emotion harms you, the other person involved, and the relationship.

Suppose your husband or boyfriend criticizes you for overcooking the turkey he won in the company raffle. He makes an insensitive comment such as, "it's as dry as a bone." Your most effective communication might be something like, "Ouch, that really hurt. In the future, I'd appreciate it if you'd keep a criticism like that to yourself." Ah, but this isn't easy when you are in the moment and upset that he would talk to you that way. It's hard not to come back with something like, "Cook it yourself next time, you jerk!" Of course, it's better to keep that bullet in the chamber because now things have escalated and it doesn't matter who started it. Nastiness begets nastiness!

This also holds true for fear. Rather than say "I'm frightened," or "You scared me," we put on a show of anger. Men in our culture are the worst offenders here, but women are not immune. Let's say you're on a ride in the mountains with a friend and she drives ten miles an hour over the speed limit and makes dangerous passes on a two-lane highway. An oncoming car could veer over the center line or a deer could bolt out at any moment. Eventually, it is bound to happen… you nearly get in an accident and you explode, "If you keep driving like a maniac, you're going to get us killed!" It would be better to make the fear primary and say, "Wow, that was close. I wonder if you'd be willing to slow down and stop passing. I get really scared." Better yet, do it before you get too frightened or almost get in an accident. This makes the point that feelings are to be used, not gotten rid of or suppressed.

Notice that you are more likely to get what you want when you make the hurt or the fear primary. When we make anger the issue, getting what you want or need is less probable. This doesn't mean you can't still express your anger, but make it secondary. Using the previous examples you could tack on a comment such as, "I get angry when you criticize my cooking. Please be more considerate in the future." Or, "It bothers me that you'd drive like that and scare me out of my wits. I'm asking you to not do it again." In both examples, the effective communicator ends up by stating clearly what they want. They don't just complain or attack, they make a clear assertion about what they need going forward and how the offender could make amends.

Amanda entered therapy wanting to know if she should stay with her husband of 35 years. They were a well-to-do couple who enjoyed boating on the Puget Sound with friends. The problem was that for Amanda and her spouse, boating involved parties with a lot of drinking, and alcohol turned Bob into a creep. After four or five drinks he would make off-color comments to her female friends and, on occasion, touch them inappropriately. Amanda was furious, and understandably so, but her primary feeling was one of embarrassment and humiliation.

Fronting with anger had gotten Amanda nowhere, Bob would yell back or stonewall her with defensiveness. When she realized her primary feeling was shame, she was able to approach him in a different way. She told her husband she was mortified when he talked and acted that way with her female friends. This got through to him and he acknowledged he had a problem and agreed to enter therapy with a counselor specializing in substance abuse. Note how much easier it is for someone to hear, "I feel so embarrassed when you act that way," as opposed to "You're acting like a creep and if you don't stop it I'm going to divorce you." The unconscious shame had to be expressed first.

Ask yourself about the feelings in you that may come before your anger, but remain beneath the surface. Be truly honest with yourself. Put a check mark next to the number and then write about these feelings until you become comfortable expressing the primary emotion. Anger is often triggered by, but actually secondary to the primary experience of:

_____   1. Fear _____

_____   2. Guilt _____

_____   3. Humiliation _____

_____   4. Rejection _____

_____   5. Hurt _____

_____   6. Discounted _____

_____   7. Ignored _____

_____   8. Insecure _____

_____   9. Not listened to _____

_____   10. Not good enough _____

_____   11. Threatened _____

_____   12. Abused _____

_____   13. Vulnerable _____

_____   14. Embarrassed _____

_____   15. Not important_____

_____   16. Found out _____

_____	**17. Out of control** _____
_____	**18. Inadequate** _____
_____	**19. Left out**_____
_____	**20. Any other feeling that comes before anger** _____

Note if a particular emotion comes up more than once, there may be an issue to deal with. Take notice and consider getting counseling if you cannot change that trigger point.

We've been talking about when we come out with anger even though some other feeling is primary. But sometimes it's the anger that's hidden from consciousness. When anger is secondary to some other emotion, we look deeper for what is primary. Hidden anger is usually the result of not getting our needs met, suffering an emotional wound, or having someone intrude upon our personal space. At other times, we hide anger for fear of retribution. It's just not safe to express anger. By hiding anger from ourselves we betray our inner voice of authenticity. Family-of-origin modeling and culture teach us to hide angry feelings, especially women, but this hurts us on many levels – personal, physical, emotional, spiritual and relational.

Beneath The Surface Of Anger Worksheet

Below is a checklist of the 50 most common signs of hidden, unexpressed anger.

1. ___ Habitual lateness.
2. ___ Enjoying biting humor.
3. ___ Sarcasm, cynicism, "flippant" conversation.
4. ___ Procrastination in finishing imposed tasks.
5. ___ Smiling while hurting inside.
6. ___ Over-controlled monotone speaking voice, or loud voice.
7. ___ Passive-aggressiveness.
8. ___ Passive resistance (slowing down of movements).
9. ___ Difficulty getting to sleep or not sleeping through the night.
10. ___ Repetitive disturbing or frightening dreams.
11. ___ Grinding teeth, especially when sleeping.
12. ___ Clenched jaw including when sleeping.
13. ___ Fist clenching, foot tapping and facial tics.
14. ___ Stomach problems.
15. ___ Overeating, or eating less.
16. ___ Frequent accidents.
17. ___ Stiff or sore neck and shoulders, backache, headache.
18. ___ Chronic depression.
19. ___ Feeling despair or discouraged.
20. ___ Suicidal thoughts.
21. ___ Lack of interest in life, including favorite pastimes.
22. ___ Boredom.
23. ___ Excessive impatience or irritability.
24. ___ Obsessing or not letting go of unfair situations.

25. ___ Regularly feeling victimized.
26. ___ Frequently feeling inadequate.
27. ___ Frequently feeling powerless.
28. ___ Frequently feeling humiliated.
29. ___ Frequently feeling ignored or "not-listened to."
30. ___ Frequently feeling unappreciated.
31. ___ Detached, feeling disconnected from other people.
32. ___ Frequent breakups or divorces.
33. ___ Nursing grievances.
34. ___ Physically/verbally hurting someone unintentionally.
35. ___ Frequently feeling guilty.
36. ___ Road anger or road rage.
37. ___ Checking out, not being present.
38. ___ Frequent crying.
39. ___ Frequent swearing.
40. ___ Frequent altercations with others.
41. ___ Frequent speeding or traffic tickets.
42. ___ Frequent lawsuits.
43. ___ Frequently feeling threatened.
44. ___ Frequently fearful.
45. ___ Not getting along with co-workers, bosses or friends.
46. ___Frequent job turnover.
47. ___Self-loathing.
48. ___Frequent negative thinking about life and others.
49. ___Wanting to break something.
50. ___Excessive use of alcohol or other substances.

This checklist may represent symptoms of other mental or medical conditions, but five or more checkmarks usually indicates hidden anger. Please consult a mental health counselor or physician if ever in doubt. Otherwise, own your anger, express it appropriately and use it as a tool for more effective coping. And by appropriately I mean your expression of anger should be skillful, well intentioned, well modulated, useful and timely.

32
Setting Limits And Graciously Educating About Boundaries

Setting limits and boundaries are an investment into a relationship.

—Anonymous

Tact is the ability to tell someone to go to hell in such a way that they look forward to the trip.

—Winston Churchill

Establishing a personal boundary is how we define ourselves in relation to others. It draws a line where I'm on one side with who I am and someone else with who they are on the other. Healthy boundaries are important in every kind of relationship, with our spouses, children, friends, co-workers, and strangers. If we're going to have meaningful, satisfying and safe relationships, we have to be able to define boundaries and set limits. To do this properly, we must be clear about who we are and what we stand for, as well as what we won't stand for.

Establishing boundaries requires that we "show up;" that is, we have to express our authentic thoughts, feelings, and needs. To do so graciously means we must be both tactful and, if not kind, at least not unkind. Sounds easy, but it isn't because we often have to tell the other the consequences of not respecting our boundary. A consequence tells the other, "I have drawn a line in the sand. If you step over it, thus and so will happen." An example in conversation with a friend would be, "I enjoy our relationship, but you blew up my phone with fifteen texts yesterday. One or two is okay, but any more than that and I feel intruded on. Please respect my limit, or

I'll have to reconsider texting with you." Or, to a new boyfriend, "I know you don't mean any harm, but I really don't like it when we French kiss in public. Call me old fashioned, but it's way outside my comfort zone. If you continue to do it, it's going to be a deal breaker!"

Sadly, women are known for not setting limits in situations where they need to. This results in a host of negative feelings. Not setting limits is partly cultural in that little girls are trained to take care of everyone and also to try to keep others happy. Not only is this a complete impossibility, but it leads to resentment, anger, anxiety and depression, and ultimately stress overload and health problems. It is also the basis for codependency, where women (men, too, but not as frequently) put their own needs on the back burner.

If you have suffered in this way, or if you've bought into the "Wonder Woman" ideal, you'd be well advised to learn to say "no." *No* is a complete sentence, an answer that will define your boundary and set a limit in situations where you feel prevailed upon. Let's say your mother-in-law asks you to host Thanksgiving at your home because "you've done such a marvelous job the last three years!" You know you don't want to. You've been under a lot of stress at work, your son was just in trouble at school for plagiarizing a book report on *Moby Dick,* and your father-in-law became intoxicated at last year's Thanksgiving and complained about the turkey being over-cooked. Say no! If you don't have it in you, practice with a friend until you wire in some new brain circuits. If that doesn't work, get a therapist and learn how to advocate for yourself.

I have a young client, call her Jamie, who has a female friend who "hangs out" at Jamie's apartment once or twice a week. The friend, without fail, and without asking, helps herself to food and drink from the refrigerator. Leftovers, milk, sodas, fruit, and vegetables – nothing is safe. Jamie is "dumbfounded" that anyone would be "so rude and clueless" to do such a thing. I, on the other hand, am not, as it seems to me that many people are poorly mannered. Trying to keep things playful, I asked Jamie the following multiple-choice question. Should you:

1. **Pretend to be away when your friend comes by?**
2. **Offer to meet her away from home at a restaurant?**

3. **Put a lock on the refrigerator?**
4. **Pretend nothing is wrong and accumulate more resentment?**
5. **Establish a boundary by being more real with her?**

The choices elicited a laugh from Jamie, but she settled on number 5. Then we put our heads together and co-authored a message for the next time the friend came over. It went like this: "I enjoy your company, but I have to tell you I don't like it when you help yourself to my food. I'm on a pretty tight budget, so I'd appreciate it if you'd stay out of my fridge. If you can't agree to that, then we'll have to meet elsewhere." We also considered, an "ask me first" approach and also a "you'll have to restock what you take," but decided the friend was so socially ignorant that the best route was to, in essence, say "no food."

At our next session I learned that Jamie set her limits as rehearsed and the friend reacted by saying, "I can't believe you'd make such a big deal out of this." Not surprising, as people with unhealthy boundaries don't typically accept it when someone sets limits with them. Jamie, having been prepared for this possibility, responded thusly, "I like you and I want to continue spending time together, but the food issue really bothers me. Maybe it shouldn't, but it does. Are you willing to accept the limits I set, or not?" The friend grumbled, but accepted Jamie's terms. The next time she came over, she brought a snack and two sodas. They got along better than they had in a long time.

Again, not everyone accepts boundaries and limits in a constructive fashion. Because some people don't "get" boundary and limit setting, they will think you are petty, controlling, judgmental, critical, offensive, abandoning, or rejecting. In fact, setting limits is none of these if done graciously and skillfully, and you needn't feel guilty. The big question is, are you willing to take a chance of "showing up" and authentically asserting your boundaries and limits? If the person in question is willing to respect and honor you, they will hear you and understand you better.

Gina has a girlfriend she has known since grade school. Every time they get together, her girlfriend rambles on about herself and her problems.

Gina resents this, as she is expected to be supportive, but is never allowed to share her own life struggles. As a result, Gina doesn't want to spend the time together that they used to. Here are a few of her choices:

1. **Gina can avoid her friend.**
2. **Gina can accept the status quo and build more resentment.**
3. **Gina could steer her friend in the direction of other subjects.**
4. **Gina can repeatedly complain to friends and me about the problem.**
5. **Gina could end the long-term friendship.**
6. **Gina can graciously establish a boundary.**

Actually, Gina tried all of the above except numbers 5 and 6. She avoided her friend by telling her she was too busy to meet. She tried to accept her friend as a "wounded sister," but only felt more resentful. She tried to steer conversations away from her friend, but it always came back to the friend talking about herself. And, God knows, she complained endlessly to everyone about her friend's pattern. Finally, she decided to opt to establish a boundary.

Gina started with a self-supportive statement about what she was feeling and then threw in the "spoonful of sugar" approach. Remember, this is saying something positive or constructive about the person or relationship, then sandwiching the boundary being set, then finishing the statement with another positive remark. It ended up like this. "This is hard for me to say to you because we've been friends our whole lives and I adore you. But I have to say that when we talk the conversation focuses almost exclusively on you. I'd like to get some airtime, too. You can be a good listener, and I need your support just as much as you need mine. Can you hear me and make a change?" The friend was taken aback, but had the integrity to acknowledge that others have given her the same feedback. Still, she occasionally reverts to form, and Gina has to remind her that she needs some talk time as well. Gina has to cue her by saying "talk time, "air time," or making a sign with her hand, as they'd mutually agreed upon these cues ahead of time. The relationship has changed for the better.

There are many kinds of boundaries and limits we need to address. To name a few there is personal space, touch, personal items, personal time, mail, noise, property lines, money, religion, politics, and sexual behavior. If you are feeling violated in regard to any of these situations, then more than likely someone has ignored or crossed your boundaries. The antidote is always to graciously establish a boundary and see if the other person will honor it. It's a litmus test. If they do, the friendship actually grows because there's more safety and trust. If not, you know they're not equipped to be the kind of friend you need.

Setting Limits And Graciously Educating About Boundaries Worksheet

1. Problem:

_____
_____
_____
_____

2. Options to say or do:

_____
_____
_____

3. Practice what you've decided to do with someone safe:

_____
_____
_____

4. Set place:

_____

5. Set time:

_____

6. Cue (build in a non-offending cue that both will agree to):

_____
_____
_____

33
A Spoonful Of Sugar

Just a spoonful of sugar helps the medicine go down In a most delightful way.

—from Mary Poppins

Keep your words soft and tender,
Because tomorrow you may have to eat them.

—Unknown

As you may or may not know, the fictional character Mary Poppins from the 1964 musical of the same name was "practically perfect in every way." Mary comes down from the clouds to help troubled children and serves as a role model for the adults who observe her cheerful attitude. Her admonition to use "a spoonful of sugar" when communicating reflects her kind and gentle character, but also her ability to be firm when needing to use authority. Remembering her advice is important whenever you're expressing a feeling or need, making a suggestion, conveying advice, giving feedback, making a point or setting a boundary.

The "spoonful" approach is especially helpful when the person you're communicating with is known to be emotionally sensitive or likely to become defensive. This skill requires kindness, compassion, consideration and respect for the other person. It is not a license to manipulate, act phony, or use a cloyingly sweet tone to get what you want or need. Think in terms of a beginning statement that is kind and complimentary, a central message that delivers your main point, and an ending statement that is positive and optimistic. Some examples will illustrate:

- **Wife to husband:** "Thanks for listening to me about my problem at work. I can tell you want what's best for me. What feels *most* supportive is when you just listen, not when you offer advice or tell me what you think I should do. It really helps knowing you're always in my corner and willing to listen."

- **Parent to child:** "You did a terrific job cleaning up this part of your room. Now I want you to pick up all your dirty clothes and place them in the hamper. Again, you did a great job getting rid of all the clutter, and I'm pleased with all the effort you've shown."

- **Friend to friend:** "Because I so value our friendship, there's something I need to say to you. In the future, please ask me before you borrow my clothes, my car, or anything else. I wouldn't ask this if I didn't want you to remain a good friend."

- **Boss to employee:** "You're doing a very thorough job on that difficult Penske file (with apologies to TV's George Costanza). You also need to include the information from the Friday brainstorming session. I'm confident the finished product will be just what we were looking for."

- **Student to professor:** "Your lectures are quite thought provoking. Could you also elaborate on this subject, as I'm still not clear on it? I'll look forward to class on Tuesday as I'm really eager to hear your explanation."

- **Neighbor to neighbor:** "I'm glad to meet you and to have a chance to talk. Please don't cut down any more of our bushes without checking with us first. I know you said you were unclear about the property line so let's walk it now, then we'll know who owns what. I look forward to being good neighbors and having a trusting relationship."

A Spoonful Of Sugar Worksheet

Assess the situation thoroughly and prepare a "spoonful of sugar" to deliver your message skillfully, without mobilizing the other's defenses or sensitivities.

1. Situation:

_____

_____

_____

2. Beginning Statement:

_____

_____

_____

_____

_____

_____

3. Central Message:

_____

_____

_____

_____

_____

_____

4. Ending Statement:

_____

_____

_____

_____

_____

5. Repeat if necessary.

Some call this skill the "Reverse Oreo" – graciousness (frosting) on the outsides and the central message (cookie) on the inside.

34
The Art Of Saying No

Be who you are and say what you feel because those who mind don't matter and those who matter don't mind.

—Dr. Seuss

One of the most important things to do when saying no is to not over explain. It leaves you wide open for someone to manipulate you. Don't give any more information than necessary. You are not a five-year-old child in the principal's office having to explain. People who want to please, avoid conflict, or have a low self-esteem are inclined to do this. It only makes the situation worse.

Here are some great examples for saying no:

1. **A spoonful of sugar:** As you have just learned, a little bit of sugar at the front end and back end can go a long way. Situation: You have great plans to go out for the evening and a friend calls and says they need a baby sitter urgently for that evening. Response: "You are a great friend. I'd love to help you but I can't. We already have plans. Why don't you try your other friends or family? I hope you find someone. I know how much this evening means to you."

2. **No, but you are open to negotiate**. Situation: My daughter has chores to do on Saturday, but she wants to spend the day with friends. Response: I say no but ask her if she is willing to get them done before Saturday so she can spend the day with her friends. If she does I would be open for her to see her friends.

3. **Saying no will be in their best interest**. Situation: A colleague asked me if there were any office spaces available in my building. Her personality would not be a good match to be in the building. Response: "It would not be a good mix. I think the personalities would not be a good match for you. Why not try some other options where you would be happier."

4. **Stating no when someone gets too personal**. Situation: I have service dogs that work in my practice with me. Sometimes clients or other people will ask me how much they cost. Response: I say to them: "It's wonderful that you like my dogs, but I don't discuss how much they cost. However, this breed of dog is listed on the Internet if you wish to learn more about them."

5. **Saying no and redirect**. Situation: A girlfriend of mine likes to come for lunch and has not offered to reciprocate. We are getting together again. She calls and says let's do it at my house again. Response: I say to her, "I haven't seen your home and garden for quite awhile. I'd like to come to your place. When is a good time?" If she says she can't because the house is not ready, or clean, or some other excuse. Then say, "We can wait until it is." Get a firm commitment to go to her house the next time or go out to eat.

Saying no can be a gracious art of educating others, setting boundaries, and developing healthy relationships. It is important to know yourself and what your needs and boundaries are. You will project confidence and sureness if you do. You are less likely to be manipulated or victimized if you come from a confident place. Direct eye contact, a firm handshake, and a steady voice always helps. Come from your Inner Adult, not your Inner Child. If someone doesn't take no the first time, then repeat one of the above options a second time. If they don't get what you are saying, then it is time to change the subject, walk away, say you have to go and hang up the phone, and so on. Again, don't over explain or apologize. Keep it simple.

35
Learning To Disengage

Well-timed silence hath more eloquence than speech.

—Martin Farquhar

Try to be mindful, and let things take their natural course. Then your mind will become still in any surroundings, like a clear forest pool. All kinds of wonderful, rare animals will come to drink at the pool, and you will clearly see the nature of all things. You will see many strange and wonderful things come and go, but you will be still.

—Achaan Chah

An important communication skill is knowing how to end a conversation when you become aware of feeling overly uncomfortable or anxious. Sometimes this happens because the communication is unproductive, sometimes because the dialogue is either off-topic or inappropriate. Maybe you need to get away, maybe you're bored to tears, maybe the stress is too much, or maybe emotions are escalating. In any event, you need the conversation to end but you want to do it in a way that is courteous and respectful.

Feel awkward or caught if you want to disengage but don't know how? Many women do, because they often stay in such conversations even though they want out. In conversations with women both in and out of treatment, I've concluded there are several reasons for staying too long in conversations we ought to exit. The first is that many of us are too polite and afraid of coming across as rude or hurtful. Another reason is sheer confusion—we simply don't know what to say or do to escape. Neither is a good reason for continuing in a conversation that is either anxiety provoking or going nowhere. That is just another way of losing power.

Some experts on communication suggest a proper ending strategy is to make a positive comment before taking leave, especially in a situation with someone you don't know well. For example, "It's been really nice to meet you, Jason, but I have to meet a girlfriend to plan a wedding shower." If you feel this strategy is deceitful, you can say instead, "I have an obligation," (to take care of yourself) without explaining. If you were in a situation where you'd just met someone and felt threatened in some way, it's a good out. You shouldn't need an out, you should be able to say "excuse me" and leave because you don't owe anyone an explanation, but sometimes too much honesty could get you in trouble. Keep in mind the words of psychoanalyst Carl Jung, "It's better to be wise than good." This is never more true than when your safety or sanity is being threatened.

Another out is to propose an action plan as a way of signaling you're about done talking. Suppose your boyfriend insists that you take a week-long summer vacation to Las Vegas. Nothing wrong with that, but it's hotter than all-get-out in Vegas in the summer, and last year you went and he lost two thousand dollars playing the slots. You've raised these concerns and he became agitated and accused you of always having to be in control. Now you're uncomfortable and want a cool down period before resuming the conversation. So you say, "Okay, I've got that this is what you want to do and you think it will be fun. I'm not so sure. I'm going to phone my travel agent tomorrow and come up with an alternate plan for us to consider." Your wrap-up and action step signals the end of conversation for the time being. When he's cooled off, he's more amenable to going somewhere that makes more sense.

When my husband and I were deciding where to put the fence line on our farm, we had a lot of energy on the subject. We were both very emotionally invested as to where it would go and our ideas rarely coincided. We ultimately decided by walking the property in small increments and negotiating the line as we went along. When either of us found ourselves emotionally overwhelmed we agreed to say, "I'm on overload. This is all I can do for now. Let's set another time." The fence line has been in for years because we were able to quit whenever negotiations broke down and because we resumed discussions when we were more rational. We came back as many times as it took to get the goal accomplished. Problem solving works if you stay in your Adult, negotiate, disengage, and don't quit.

Kathy, a new client in her early thirties, tells me that she and her husband of ten years argue a lot. Money, sex, in-laws, kids—they seem to disagree about anything and everything. She wants to buy a new car, he argues they don't have the money. He wants sex eight days a week: she wants it once. He wants to spend holidays with his family; she can't stand his loud, alcoholic father. She wants to play good cop to the kids; he wants her to be tougher. The problem is their arguments get heated and escalate to the point that it scares the kids (not to mention the family dog). Sometimes even the neighbors get involved. I am currently teaching Kathy the art of disengaging. Here are some things she is learning to say:

1. **"I know this is important to discuss, but we're escalating.** Let's talk later."
2. **"I'm on overload/tired/irritable/starving.** It would be better to put this off for awhile."
3. **"I'd like to hear you out, but I can't focus right now.** I need to change my clothes/wash my face/sit down and rest. I can give you better attention after I take care of myself."
4. **"There is more than likely a solution to this, but now isn't working.** We can find a better solution later."
5. **"I would like to listen to you, but I'm wiped out.** I can listen better when I've had a break."
6. **"You deserve my full attention. I can't give it to you now.** Can you we do it later today or tomorrow? Let's set a time."
7. **"This is not the best time now.** I'd like to suggest we put this on the shelf until eight o'clock tomorrow night. We both need time to cool off."
8. **"I have to leave now.** Let's talk tomorrow morning at eight o'clock and set another time to give this our full attention."
9. **"Okay, I don't want to hear this.** I won't continue unless we can talk respectfully to one another. If that's not possible, let's set another time or way to communicate (telephone, e-mail, letter)."

It's always a good idea to disengage if things are escalating, because you're not going to solve anything from a position of anger. If the other person follows you from room to room, or refuses to let go of the issue, give them something to hold onto. Counteroffers work. Set another time to talk so the other doesn't feel like you're avoiding them or simply don't care. Remember to follow-up on the arranged meeting time or resentments may build up. The person who disengages is the one responsible for initiating the follow-up meeting.

The only time you don't offer another time to talk is when you wish to not speak of the subject again. Examples of this would be during times of manipulation, control, or abuse. Sometimes it's time to agree to disagree, especially if you've beat a subject to death and neither of you is going to change your mind or position. Notice it's more the way you talk about loaded or uncomfortable subjects than the actual content of the subject itself, because it's okay to disagree. You and the other are entitled to different points of view, and there is no absolute reality. The problem arises when you try to take over the other person's mind and insist they see it your way. Or, vice versa. No one's eyes are God's eyes, so respect differences. I can't tell you how many marriages could be saved if couples adopted this philosophy.

The real art of conversation is not only to say the right thing at the right place, but to leave unsaid the wrong thing at the tempting moment.
—Dorothy Nevill

Learning To Disengage Worksheet

1. Disengaging statement.

_____
_____
_____
_____
_____
_____

2. Set another time to talk.

_____
_____
_____

3. Set a time to set another time to talk.

_____
_____
_____

4. Initiating the next meeting (the person who disengages is the one to initiate the next meeting).

_____
_____
_____

5. Let go and agree to disagree.

_____
_____
_____

6. Repeat as many times as it takes to resolve the issue.

_____

_____

_____

36
Handling Annoying People

Never argue with an idiot, people passing by may not know the difference.

—Mark Twain

Don't let negative and toxic people rent space in your head. Raise the rent and kick them out.

—Unknown

How then shall we respond to people who are rude, inconsiderate, or downright mean? In order to answer this question, we must first ask two others: Do you want to go through life kicking and screaming in response to people who push your buttons? Or do you want to walk in peace? The choice is yours.

Being human among humans, we are regularly subjected to the ignorance of others, not to mention their bad and boorish behavior. What is the best way to respond?

A school of psychology known as Psychosynthesis sheds light on this subject. Psychosynthesis teaches that we all have a Higher Self, a Centered Self, and a Lower Self. The Lower Self is immature, easily offended, and quick to react. It is also contagious in that when a person comes at us from their Lower Self, we are likely to catch it from them and react from ours. Contrast this to the Higher Self, which is characterized by a nonjudgmental attitude, forgiveness, and unconditional love. In between is the Centered Self, the part of us that can continue thinking under stress and respond appropriately rather than react to the bad behavior of others.

Staying in our Centered Self is a choice that allows us to ignore or avoid others who choose to behave badly. If we are in a situation that can't be ignored or avoided, we can still stay centered, but it requires both self-awareness and intention.

Example: You are standing in line to get tickets to a performance by your favorite musician when you observe a young couple crowd in front of you. The show is nearly sold out and you could conceivably get shut out as a result of their aggressive behavior. What do you do?

Lower Self: You angrily confront the couple, become engaged in a shouting match, and use language you later regret. You have descended to their level and your self-esteem plummets accordingly.

Centered Self: You politely inform the couple that the end of the line is "back there." When they ignore you, you find someone who works at the venue and ask them to deal with the situation. You feel anxious and upset, but strive to remain calm.

Higher Self: You politely inform the couple that the end of the line is "back there." When they ignore you, you find someone who works at the venue and ask them to deal with the situation. You watch your feelings as if a detached observer and remain at peace. You pray for the rude couple or at least feel compassion for them, knowing they are behaving in ways that will attract negative energy and bad consequences.

Finally, notice your self-talk as you deal with and experience rude or difficult people. Ask yourself: "Is this situation worth getting angry over?" "Am I going to give this person power over my mental health?" Then, tell yourself, "This situation is not going to last forever; I will be out of this soon." Or, "Let go of your feelings about this person and focus on something else." Remember to breathe. Pray for peace. Choose to stay in your Centered Self. Be free.

37
Effective Praise

The more you praise and celebrate your life, the more there is in life to celebrate.
—Oprah Winfrey

Praise invariably implies a reference to a higher standard.
—Aristotle

Praise is like oxygen. We all need it, and we don't stop needing it just because we're no longer children. Jack Canfield, of *Chicken Soup for the Soul* fame, cites a study in which two-year-olds were followed around for a day and found that the average child received approximately fifteen negative comments for every positive one. Is it any wonder we still want and need praise?

Below is a list of ways to praise children, other people in your life, and yourself. Note that praise is given for specific actions rather than general character. Read the list, you'll get the idea.

Parent to child: "Since you put so much effort into your science project, you're going to raise your grade." Rather than, "You're a smart kid!"

"I'm so pleased to see you studying your multiplication flash cards again. You're on the right track now." Rather than, "You're super!"

You to a co-worker: "A month ago you didn't know how to use the computer program, but now you've practiced and you're fully up to speed. That's great!" Rather than, "You're a real asset!"

"I noticed how you took time to introduce our new employee to everyone in the office. I'm certain she appreciated your thoughtfulness. How impressive!" Rather than, "You're the best!"

You to self: "You studied hard for the bar exam and now you've passed the test. You're going to make an excellent attorney." Rather than, "Great job!"

"Your landscape design is a creative and beautiful use of space. Top-notch work!" Rather than, "You're the greatest!"

The idea is to water the flowers rather than the weeds and to make the praise specific in order to make it effective. This form of praise is a coping skill because it helps us to relate successfully with others and also because it encourages us to respond to the challenges of our own lives. Learn to say to yourself what you would say to your best friend when they deserve praise. Try it on your kids, yourself, and everyone with whom you come in contact. It works!

Suggestions for praise:

1. **"You've put in a full day today."** (list examples)_____
2. **"Your work has such personality."** (list examples)_____
3. **"That's very perceptive."** (list examples)_____
4. **"Your remark shows a lot of sensitivity."** (list examples)_____
5. **"I noticed that you got right down to work."** (list examples)_____
6. **"You've really been paying attention."** (explain why)_____
7. **"That's quite an improvement."** (list examples)_____
8. **"That's an interesting way of looking at it."** (explain why)_____
9. **"Good reasoning."** (list examples) _____
10. **"Superior work"** (list examples)_____
11. **"That's a very good observation."** (list why)_____
12. **"Nice going."** (list why)_____
13. **"This shows you've been thinking."** (list why)_____

14. "Beautiful." (list why)_____

15. "Excellent work." (list examples)_____

16. "You've come a long way with this one." (list why)_____

17. "I appreciate your help." (list examples)_____

18. "A splendid job." (list why)_____

19. "I like the way you've handled this." (list why)_____

20. "You're right on the mark." (list why)_____

21. "This is quite an accomplishment." (explain why)_____

22. "Good thinking." (list examples)_____

23. "Job well done." (list examples)_____

24. "I like the way you are working today." (explain why)_____

25. "How impressive." (explain why)_____

26. "This really has flair." (explain why)_____

27. "Terrific." (explain why)_____

28. "Thank you." (explain why)_____

29. "You've made my day." (explain why)_____

30. "This is something special." (list examples)_____

38
Accepting Compliments

I can live for two months on a good compliment.

—Mark Twain

A compliment is a gift, not to be thrown away carelessly, unless you want to hurt the giver.

—Eleanor Hamilton

Some of us have a hard time accepting compliments. Women, even more than men. Perhaps women are conditioned to be more modest. Not taking it in is often an indicator of low self-esteem. Because the compliment clashes with our less-than-positive view of ourselves, we reject it, as well as the person who delivered it.

For example, an attentive husband tells his wife how beautiful and sexy she looks in her new evening dress. Having gained twenty pounds and several dress sizes, she responds, "Oh, you're just saying that." She rejects the compliment because it doesn't fit with her body image of a woman who has become overweight. If she could take it in and allow her husband's words to nurture her, the compliment might make her happy. By deflecting the compliment she keeps herself emotionally unfulfilled.

To learn the art of accepting a compliment, practice the following steps:

1. **Smile, take a deep breath and make a conscious effort to take it in.**
2. **Make eye contact and thank the person who issued the compliment.**
3. **Avoid diluting the compliment by immediately turning around and issuing one to the person who complimented you.**

4. **Resist the temptation to dispute the compliment, even if you have difficulty taking it in.**
5. **Savor the compliment and watch your self-esteem and self-confidence grow by leaps and bounds.**

Over time, you'll begin to feel better about yourself and taking compliments will become more natural. Try it. It works.

39
What's In A Handshake?

I can feel the twinkle of his eye in his handshake.

—Helen Keller

That is very important. The weak, horrible, wet fish handshake is a problem. That gives a lot away.

—Diana Mather

Marlee Matlin won the Academy Award for best actress in *Children of a Lesser God*, her film debut. Marlee is almost completely deaf after a bout with roseola infantum at the age of eighteen months. But she never let that hold her back personally or professionally. Barely verbal because of the disability, Marlee, perhaps better than anyone, knows the value of making a good first impression. It is no wonder she is said to have the best handshake in Hollywood.

Possession of a good handshake is not a coping skill per se, but it's included here because of its immense importance as a social skill. If you're trying to make a good first impression with a person you've just met and give them a "crusher" handshake, chances are you've already blown the relationship. If you're trying to land a new job and you give your prospective boss a "dead fish" handshake, well, let's just say your stock went down in comparison to other applicants. An impressive handshake will not only get you off to a good start, but will also set the tone for a positive ongoing relationship.

Appropriate handshakes and greeting rituals vary from culture to culture, but in the West, there are a few easy rules to follow that will keep you in good stead (my father, a successful attorney, taught me these when I was a little girl):

1. **Walk right up to the person** whose hand you will shake.
2. **Make eye contact** and hold it in a friendly way, but don't stare.
3. **Reach your right hand out:** don't wait for the other person to do it first.
4. **Give them a firm grip,** as if you were holding a hammer.
5. **Give them two or three subtle up-and-down strokes.**
6. **If you want to give a more intimate handshake, let it linger.**
7. **To show extra friendliness, place your left hand on the hand you are shaking** or do the "Bill Clinton" Presidential handshake by using your left hand to gently touch the other person's elbow.

Here are a few things to say when shaking hands:

1. **"Nice to meet you."**
2. **"How are you?"**
3. **"Hello!"**
4. **"It's good to finally meet you. I've heard good things about you."**
5. **"You're looking well. It's good to see you again."**
6. **"Diana Lee. Pleased to meet you."**

This chapter may seem intuitively obvious to most readers, yet proper handshaking is a lost art, and I never cease to be amazed at how people's poor social skills undermine them personally and professionally. People aren't likely to forget a weak, wet, or limp handshake. Conversely, they will remember your firm, warm, professional handshake and judge you as a person of substance. Proper handshaking is one of the single most important things you can do when you're meeting someone new, on a first date, presenting yourself at a job interview, networking, or greeting people in any other situation. Practice the steps above and notice how you are taken more seriously.

40
Front-End, Back-End Work

There is no such thing as luck, just preparedness and opportunity.
—Benjamin Franklin

For most of my younger life, I believed life was like a sitcom. As the main character in my real-life drama, I had to be clever and capable of catching everything perfectly at the "front-end." Whether conversing with a client or chatting over the fence with my neighbor, I needed to provide wise counsel or come up with a witty comeback on the spot. Similarly, I had to flawlessly screen people who are unsafe, unhealthy, or a bad match. My sitcom "icon" would have a ready and perfect plan for any situation. Unable to fulfill such lofty expectations, I came to accept my imperfections. Yes, I could occasionally bring my "A-game," but I couldn't consistently catch everything at the front-end. No one can.

Front-end work is valuable and can be developed through experience, learning, education, and training, but it's impossible to catch it all on life's first take. This should come as a great relief, because many of us feel shame and beat ourselves up if we don't get it in the initial phase. As most of us have learned the hard way, making sound decisions usually requires that we take a series of steps before committing to a certain course of action.

Sitting with unfinished business and taking time to process a problem or issue is "back-end" work. Back-end work is not only okay, it is often more effective because it gives us time to think so we can learn how to do things differently. Specifically, if we decide to go back and revisit a conversation or situation, we may now plan what to say or do, as well as pick an optimal place and time. Moreover, with back-end work there is less room for shame and guilt, more room for creative planning and problem solving that can be applied to the present situation. This creates transferable skills that may be applied to new and future situations. This is very powerful.

This example involves limit setting. A childhood friend brought her son to my home for a "first visit." After entering my home, this preschooler invaded every space and began handling personal items without regard to their fragile and valuable nature. Though I expected my friend to supervise her little boy, she sat idly while I ran interference. Finally, putting item after item out of reach and telling her son no, I said in frustration, "Would you please stop him from doing this?"

She replied, "This wouldn't be a problem if you didn't live in a museum." Dismayed by her disrespect and fearing for the safety of my belongings, I cut the visit short.

Front-end: I wish I had said something prior to the visit about her son needing close supervision. I wish I'd come up with a wise and gracious response to her comment about "living in a museum." But would either have made a difference? I think not.

Back-end: After replaying the scene in my mind, I realized there wasn't much I could have said that would have made any difference. I later discovered her son's behavior, as well as her lack of supervision and training, was consistent in every social circumstance. I also accepted that just because I have a long-term childhood friend, it does not mean she would share my belief that children should be raised with an understanding of boundaries and respect for other people's property. If she doesn't get it, why would her child?!

I asked myself if it was worth it to discuss this matter in regard to future visits to my home. Because I wanted to see my friend again, it became important to set limits regarding her son. I thought carefully about how to tell her in a way that would be least likely to elicit another round of her defensiveness. I phoned and told her she was correct that my home, because of all the knick-knacks and collectibles from my travels, it was not kid-friendly. I confessed I felt anxious about him breaking something of value to my husband or me. I said I cared about her and wanted to continue to meet; however, if she could not guarantee close supervision of her son, we would have to meet somewhere other than my home. She told me she was unwilling to make the guarantee so, from that point on, we met at restaurants without her son. Thereafter, we rarely met and, sadly, our friendship was never the same again.

Maxine, a client in her forties, complained that her mother treated her like a child. It had always been this way, even after graduating college with honors and becoming a successful speech pathologist. Maxine had no idea how to step out of this role, or what to say in response to her mother's constant advice and criticism. She was convinced her mother didn't think she could do anything right. I told my client I believed her mother loved her and wanted the best for her. The problem was she was unaware of how her delivery affected Maxine's self-esteem.

Front-end: Maxine and I co-created some readymade responses. When her mother offered unwanted advice, she would say, "Thank you for your care and concern. I'll give that some consideration." In response to criticism, she would offer, "Thanks for the feedback," or "I know you want what's best for me, but when you offer unwanted advice, I feel disrespected." If this doesn't bring closure, Maxine was to try changing the topic. If her mother still didn't back off, Maxine would excuse herself by leaving or getting off the phone. If her mother picked it up later, Maxine would remind her, "I appreciate your concern, but I have to be my own person so, in the future, I only want your advice when I ask for it." As adults we can pick and choose what we wish from anyone's advice or whether we get it in the first place.

Back-end: Maxine decided to pick and choose the time, place, and topic for the next meeting with her mother. She was also assigned a homework assignment of practicing staying in her Adult part. "It's like driving the team bus," I told her. "You wouldn't want a child driving the bus or you'd likely end up upside down in the ditch." Should she slip into her Child part during the course of the conversation, she was to excuse herself to the ladies room and summon the most Adult, grown-up, resourceful and womanly part of her personality. This part would then resume discussions with her mother, while the Child would sit safely in the back of the bus, observing. In the future this exercise would become front-end work.

Transferable Skill: Front-end, back-end work can also be used in the workplace with bosses or coworkers, in response to micromanagement. If you use this approach, take into account the relationship you have with the person in question and the formality or informality of the workplace environment.

Example: "Thank you for the information, your feedback is important to me." Or, "I appreciate what you said, thank you. That makes things very clear." These responses clearly come from the Professional Adult rather than the "Child Within," who may have a need to prove, defend, or rebel.

SKILLS FOR BACK-END WORK

1. **Process the situation.** For example, with yourself, a friend, a mentor, or by writing a letter you have no intention to actually mail or deliver. This will reduce the energy of feelings in order to think, problem solve, and communicate effectively.

2. **Learn from it.** How can I apply this information in the future, as a "Transferable Skill" for front-end work?

3. **Come up with a workable solution.** Give it a try. If the situation offers no solution, either let go, find a way to live with it, or leave the circumstances.

4. **Assess the wisdom of self-expression.** Choose whether or not presenting your feelings or solution is personally therapeutic or if it will be instrumental in changing a situation. If it would hurt you, others, or the situation you are in, drop it. If the Hell's Angels crowd into the line at the theater, it might be best to not say anything.

5. **If you choose to act, do so skillfully.** This means presenting yourself in a gracious, mature, professional way, appropriate to the situation. Decide whether the best method of expression is an individual or group meeting, a letter, a telephone call, or an email. If it's face-to-

face, choosing the right place is important to ensure that the meeting be safe and productive. Depending on how safe you feel with this person, being out of the earshot of others may be a consideration. If there is a potential for violence, you will want the company of others or have someone do it for you (e.g., your disgruntled and hotheaded ex-boyfriend is coming over to pick up his possessions).

The practice of back-end work supports front-end work. Back-end work is really life experience put in practice. The transferable skills acquired directly apply to front-end work. Back-end work should not to be underestimated; indeed, it may be the most powerful work we do. Back-end work prepares us for forthcoming opportunities, and those never end.

Front-End, Back-End Work Worksheet

1. **Situation:**

   _____

   _____

   _____

2. **Process the situation (lower your energy and get clear):**

   _____

   _____

   _____

   _____

3. **What have you learned?**

   _____

   _____

   _____

   _____

4. **A workable solution:**

   _____

   _____

   _____

5. **Reasons for expressing or not (could just be therapeutic for you):**

   _____

   _____

   _____

   _____

   _____

6. **How is it going to be presented? What are you going to say and do?:**

_____

_____

_____

_____

_____

7. **In what form will it be presented (telephone, e-mail, letter, in person, or with another person present?):**

_____

_____

_____

_____

8. **The right place for back-end work (where you will feel the strongest and safest):**

_____

_____

_____

_____

9. **The right time for back-end work (opportunity where you will not be interrupted or rushed):**_____

_____

_____

_____

The Journey

One day you finally knew
what you had to do, and began,
though the voices around you
kept shouting
their bad advice –
though the whole house
began to tremble
and you felt the old tug
at your ankles.
"Mend my life!"
each voice cried.
But you didn't stop.
You knew what you had to do,
though the wind cried
with its stiff fingers
at the very foundations,
though their melancholy
was terrible.
It was already late
enough, and a wild night,
and the road full of fallen
branches and stones.
But little by little,
as you left their voices behind,
the stars began to burn
through the sheets of clouds,
and there was a new voice
which you slowly
recognized as your own,
that kept you company
as you strode deeper and deeper

into the world,
determined to do
the only thing you could do –
determined to save
the only life you could save.

—**Mary Oliver**

About The Author

Diana F. Lee is an accomplished counselor with almost four decades of experience empowering people to resolve issues and make positive changes in their lives. She emphasizes skill building and work on grief, spirituality, and creativity while collaborating with other health care professionals to facilitate improved self-worth and a balanced, spiritually based lifestyle.

Diana was born and raised in the Pacific Northwest and was a twenty-five-year resident of Snohomish, Washington. She appreciates nature and enjoyed living on a small farm that was home for horses, goats, geese, ducks, dogs, and cats. She recently moved to La Conner, Washington. She has been with her husband, William Henry Taylor, for thirty-seven years. He is a lawyer in Everett. They have a daughter, Katherine Lee Taylor, who is also an attorney.

Diana has Master's Degrees in Education/Counseling and Public Administration, and a post-master's certificate in Transforming Spirituality, all from Seattle University; she has also completed a program in counseling chemical dependency issues. She worked as a probation officer for fifteen years and has been in private practice since 1983 treating individuals, families, and couples. She has many years of group work with adults in addiction recovery. Diana is now working as a spiritual director in her Everett private practice, as well. She is a local and international speaker on mental health and addiction issues. For the last twelve years, she has used three therapy dogs in her practice.

Diana loves to travel and has been profoundly influenced by European, Asian, and Russian cultures. With her interest in spiritual growth, Diana has visited numerous temples, churches, monasteries, and other sacred sites. A lifelong lover of horses, she has ridden in most of the countries she has visited. She has many creative outlets and has held numerous art shows that included her wall hangings, photography, clothing, purses, and jewelry. She also enjoys designing gardens and homes.

About The Dogs

"Dr. Jerry," Jerome Samuel Taylor, is a great boy who has worked at the office since he was one year of age. He is thirteen years old now. He loves to go to the waiting room and greet the clients. He has been known to lick the tears off of the cheeks of clients if they wish. He quite often gets out of his bed and goes over to clients, sits by them and puts a paw on their lap or arm to comfort them. He is helpful to patients with Post Traumatic Stress Disorder and Depression. He always knows when the sessions are finished and waits quietly by the door to say goodbye.

Jack McCoy Taylor is the rebel. He is a boundary violator. He loves people and wants to be in their faces. I bring him to work when I have clients who are rebellious or need to set limits. I tell them he is a rebel and perhaps they can relate to him. I once had a client who told his story after Jack rolled over belly up on his lap. The client said, "if he can show the underside of his belly then so can I." He proceeded to tell his story. Jack also responds well to the phrase, "Where are your boundaries?" He backs up and sits down and waits patiently. Clients laugh and love it. I use him with clients to practice setting boundaries firmly without apologizing or feeling bad. They get lots of practice.

Jenny Taylor passed away in December 2010. She had a gift for treating people who were abused and molested. She would climb up on clients' laps and put a paw on them when they cried, told their story, or did "guided imagery" work. She had a way of looking into clients' eyes as if to say, "I care about you and know your pain." She was fourteen years old when she passed.

These three courageous, loving Brussels Griffons have provided wonderful, empathetic responses to clients in my work place. It is important to acknowledge their accomplishments because they have created a special, nurturing, safe place for the clients to work.

There is a mountain of research on the effectiveness of animal-assisted therapy; for example, reduced anxiety and depression, reduced loneliness, lower stress levels and improved overall health.

Made in the USA
San Bernardino, CA
18 October 2014